JUN 23 '95	NOV 28 '97	
JUN 30 '95	FEB 20 '98	
JY 28 '95	SEP 4 '98	
	NOV 6 '98	
NOV 17 '95	JUN 18	
NOV 24 '95		
DEC 01 '95		
JAN 26 '96		
FE 16 '96		
AG 02 '96		
OC 25 '96		

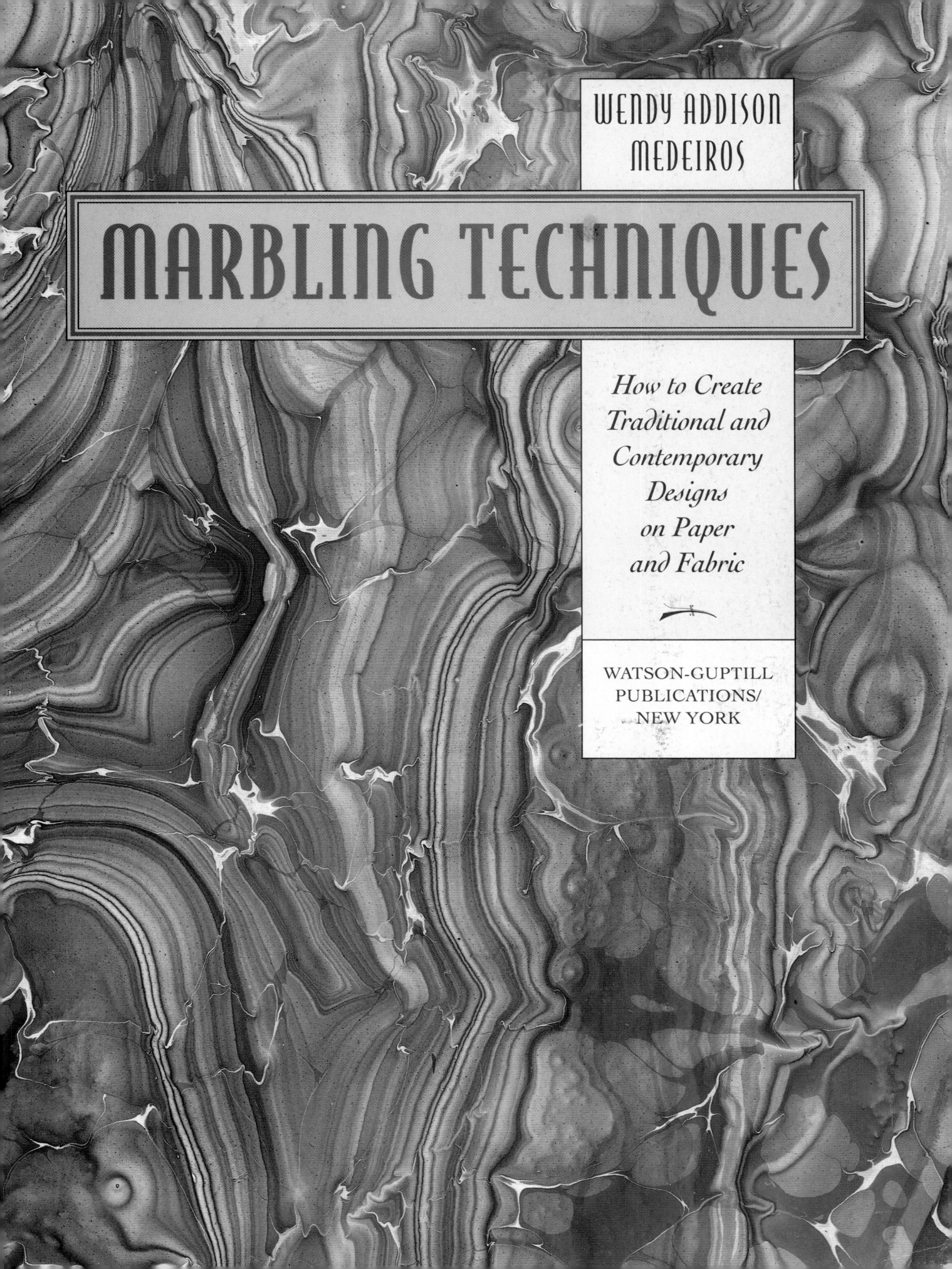

WENDY ADDISON
MEDEIROS

MARBLING TECHNIQUES

*How to Create
Traditional and
Contemporary
Designs
on Paper
and Fabric*

Watson-Guptill
Publications/
New York

Page 1: A modern Brazilian marbler, Fernando Machado, created this mesmerizing pattern by over-marbling a red and blue stone pattern with a Spanish Wave in gray.

Title page: This marbled sheet bears a deliberate resemblance to malachite. The author created this irregular Spanish Wave pattern (called the Moiré) by shifting the paper as it was slowly laid on the paints. The paper was first folded and slightly crumpled to encourage the random touch-down.

Right: The Nonpareil may tend to get somewhat darker on one side (right) as you pull the comb toward you. If this bothers you, prop the tray up on the darker end, using a pencil or a book after you have pulled the comb through. The floating paints will even themselves out.

Senior Editor: Candace Raney
Associate Editor: Dale Ramsey
Designer: Bob Fillie, Graphiti Graphics
Production Manager: Hector Campbell

Note: All marbled artwork, unless otherwise noted, is by the author.
Portions of this book are reprinted with the permission of *Ink and Gall* magazine and Savoir-Faire.

First published in 1994 in the United States by Watson-Guptill Publications,
a division of BPI Communications, Inc. 1515 Broadway, New York, New York 10036

Library of Congress Cataloging-in-Publication Data
Medeiros, Wendy Addison.
      Marbling techniques : how to create traditional and contemporary designs on
  paper and fabric / Wendy Addison Medeiros ; photography by Mitchell Allen
  Medeiros.
          p.   cm.
      Includes index.
      ISBN 0-8230-3005-9 : $24.95
      1. Marbling. 2. Marbled papers. 3. Textile painting. I. Title.
  TT385.M43 1994
  745.7—dc20   94-19095
                                                                    CIP

Manufactured in Hong Kong

1 2 3 4 5 / 98 97 96 95 94

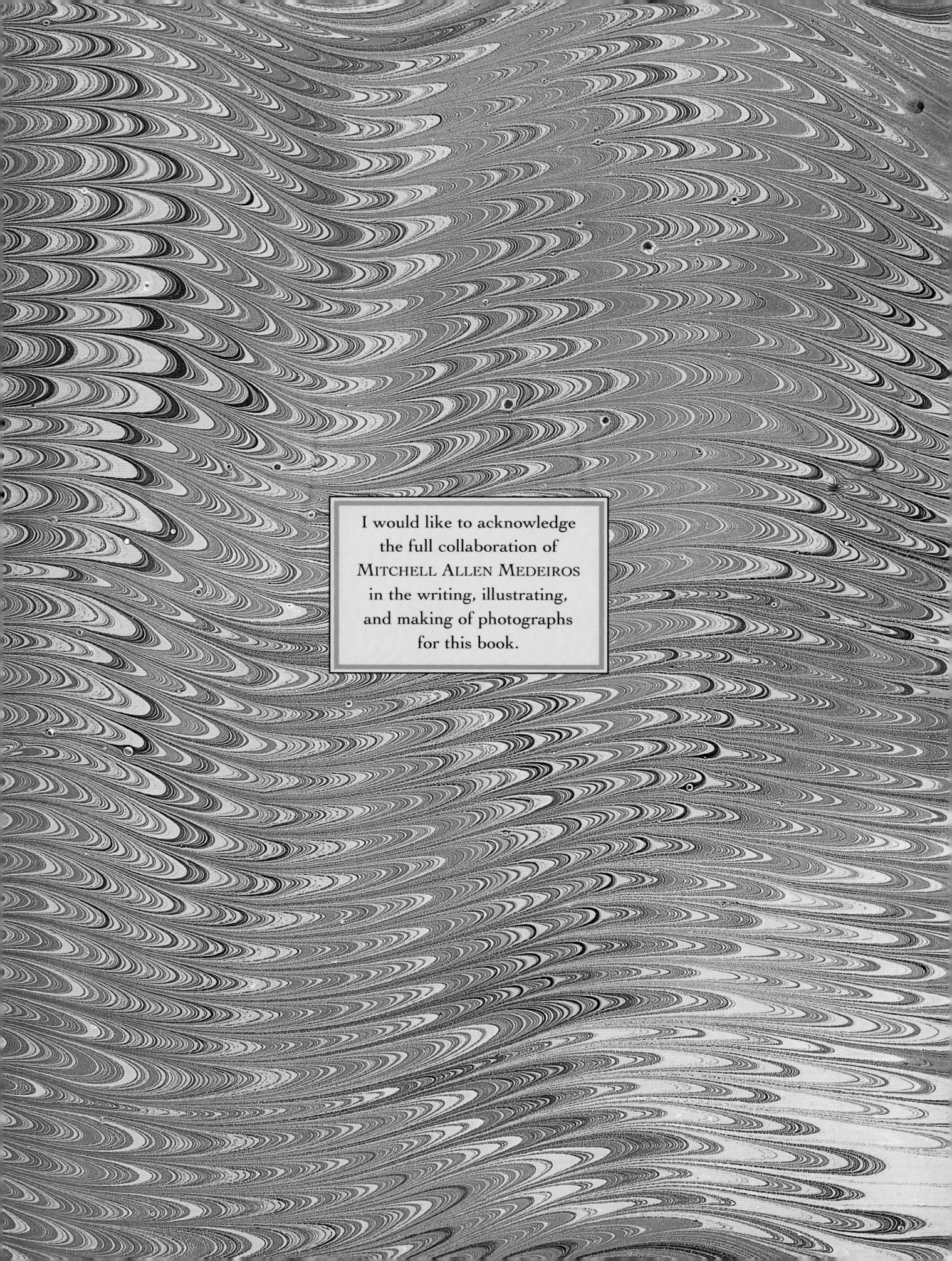

I would like to acknowledge
the full collaboration of
MITCHELL ALLEN MEDEIROS
in the writing, illustrating,
and making of photographs
for this book.

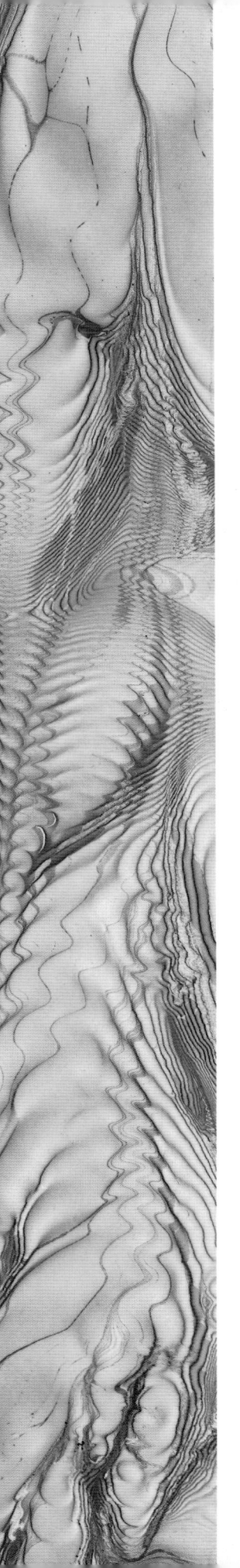

CONTENTS

THE ROMANCE OF MARBLING   9

PART ONE. PREPARING TO MARBLE   35
TOOLS FOR MARBLING   37
MATERIALS   45
USING ACRYLICS   59
USING WATERCOLOR AND GOUACHE   63
USING OIL PAINTS   67
USING TEMPERA   71
THE WORKSPACE   75

PART TWO. THE MARBLING PROCESS   79
PATTERN MAKING   81
TECHNICAL PROBLEMS   97
SPECIAL TECHNIQUES   105
MARBLING ON FABRIC   117
SUGGESTED PROJECTS   123

APPENDIX   135
MARBLING AS A BUSINESS   137
SOURCES   141

INDEX   142

THE ROMANCE OF MARBLING

for centuries, marbling was an art form found only inside the covers of books. Contemporary artists and designers have rediscovered this versatile design motif, and marbled papers are now seen everywhere, in picture frames and lamp shades, wine labels and fine art. This ancient craft, named "ebru" ("cloud art") by its 15th-century Persian practitioners, is now undergoing a renaissance. This book is designed to help you participate in this development—not to repeat yourself and others over and over, but to go beyond that and to re-invent the art of marbling in new and wonderful ways.

< An exquisite sample of Victorian marbling (around 1860) from an English encyclopedia. Collection of Olaf.

By most accounts, European-style paper marbling originated in Persia in the 1400s. The name of the first marbler is a mystery. The invention was probably an accidental one, made by some observant artist who noticed that paints would float on water. The exact formula of the earliest marblers is lost; however, the process moved, city by city, through Turkey, Spain, Italy, France, and the rest of Europe, probably along the trade routes, over the next three centuries. As it traveled, each country adapted the technique and changed the materials and recipes to accord with indigenous materials. Very few useful illustrations of these practices were ever made, and almost no instructions were written down in the earliest centuries of the craft.

In those days, a trader guarded such knowledge. Secrets were passed on only to apprentices sworn to silence, or from parents to offspring. This general attitude of propriety still exists today. Most marblers are very, very reticent about divulging their processes, their materials, and their sources, which is a major reason that marbling has remained such an esoteric craft.

In the mid-1800s, there was a general revival of interest in marbling. It became the decorative paper used by bookbinders, eclipsing the use of printed papers, paste papers, Dutch gilt, and drip marbled papers. Much credit must be given to the English, who, in the mid-1800s, published several comprehensive books on the marbling process, thus boosting it out of its secrecy and guaranteeing that the art would never die out.

Over the centuries, the art of marbling has taken on many different forms. The Turks did not use marbled papers for bookbinding, but, by using stencils, made them an element of figurative art. They would lay down a cut-paper stencil or use a block-out medium, then marble different areas with a human figure or animal. They also very effectively used marbled patterns as a framing and bordering device. Another Turkish application that was quite different from the later European uses was to create figures, animals, and flowers directly on the marbling surface using a stylus.

As marbling moved into the Mediterranean countries of Spain and Italy, it began to develop into its present form. The Italians, and especially the Venetians, picked up the art of marbling and made it a wonderful process for creating repeated patterns. To this day, the Venetians and the Florentines are famous all over the world for their marbling. From lower Europe it spread into France and on into Holland and England. Along the way, hundreds of anonymous artisans must have sweated away thousands of hours over their marbling trays trying to re-invent the process, trying to eliminate exasperating problems and to find new and better materials and methods.

This process is still going on. Today, in this country, there is a small group of experimenters still seeking the key, not to the Alchemist's Stone, but to a foolproof method of marbling. Alas, no such method will ever be found. But along the way, many a jewel will be lifted from the water, fresh and dripping, and it will be like no other sheet ever made.

For you to explore marbling and make your own successful experiments, it is essential that you understand the basic technique which, throughout all its historical variations, has never changed. The process is always the same: paints are made to float on the surface of water where they are manipulated into designs and then transferred to a sheet of paper. In order to make this happen, the artist must learn to control the behavior of the paint. The moment the paints hit the water, they will either sink to the bottom of the tray (and darken the marbler's day), or magically float and spread, enabling the marbler to coax them almost effortlessly into liquid swirls. Then paper or silk is simply laid onto the surface where it instantly picks up the floating film of paint. Thus, each sheet is a unique design created in a transfer process in which the artist is working hand in hand with the happenstance and mutability of nature. And truly, the best marbled designs reflect the watery dynamics of this craft.

I have included in the succeeding pages a master's gallery of marbled designs, old and new, to fire your imagination and to show you exactly how many different directions you can take with this process.

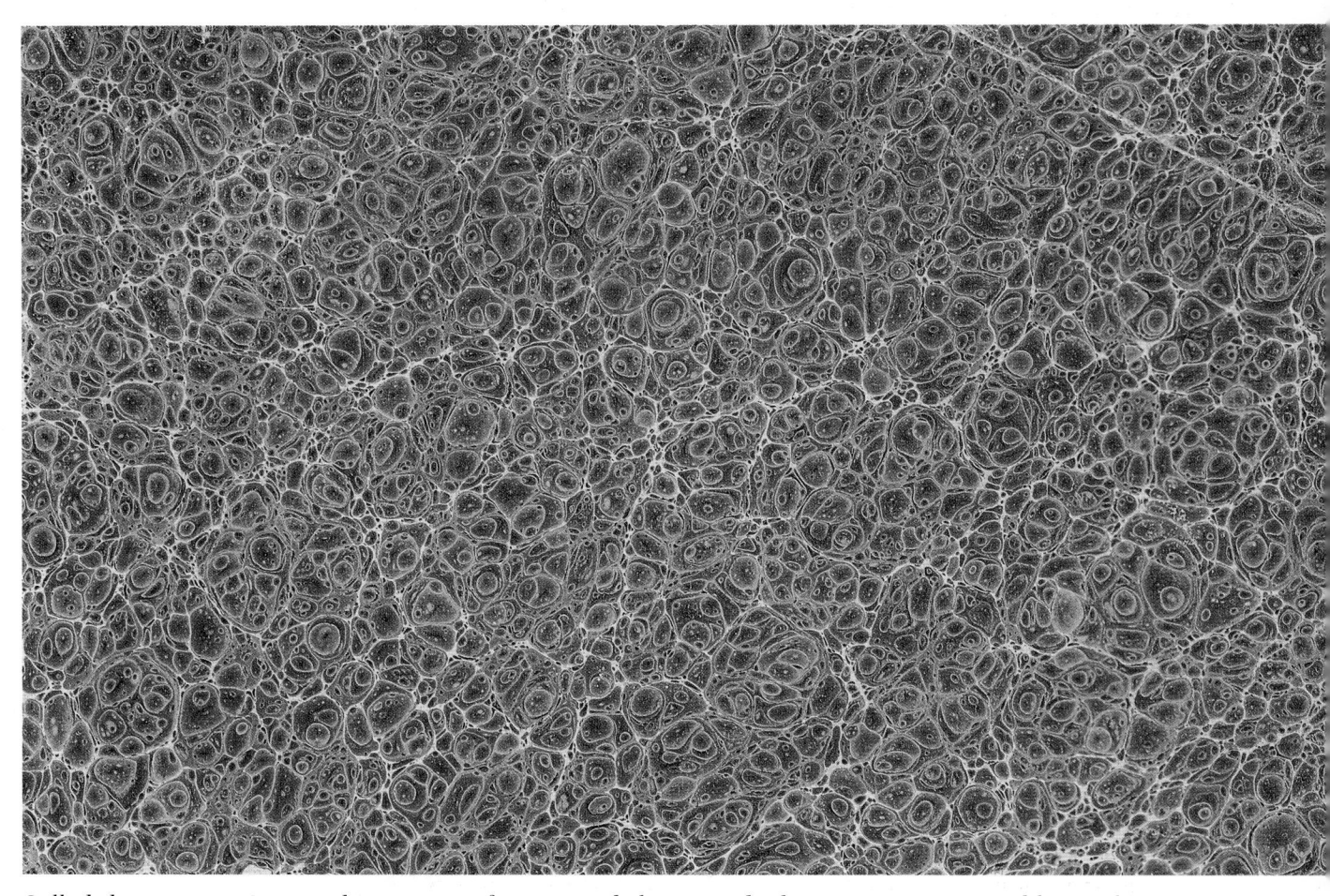

Called the FRENCH SHELL, this pattern of tiny round shapes and white veining is created by applying several layers of paint with a paint additive. Found in a book dated 1875.

∧ This antique booklining from around 1860 has
the detail so prized by professionals.

═══════════════════════════════════

> This sample of the pattern called CURTAIN dates from about 1880,
to which the artist gave a wiggle and added a SPANISH WAVE as well.

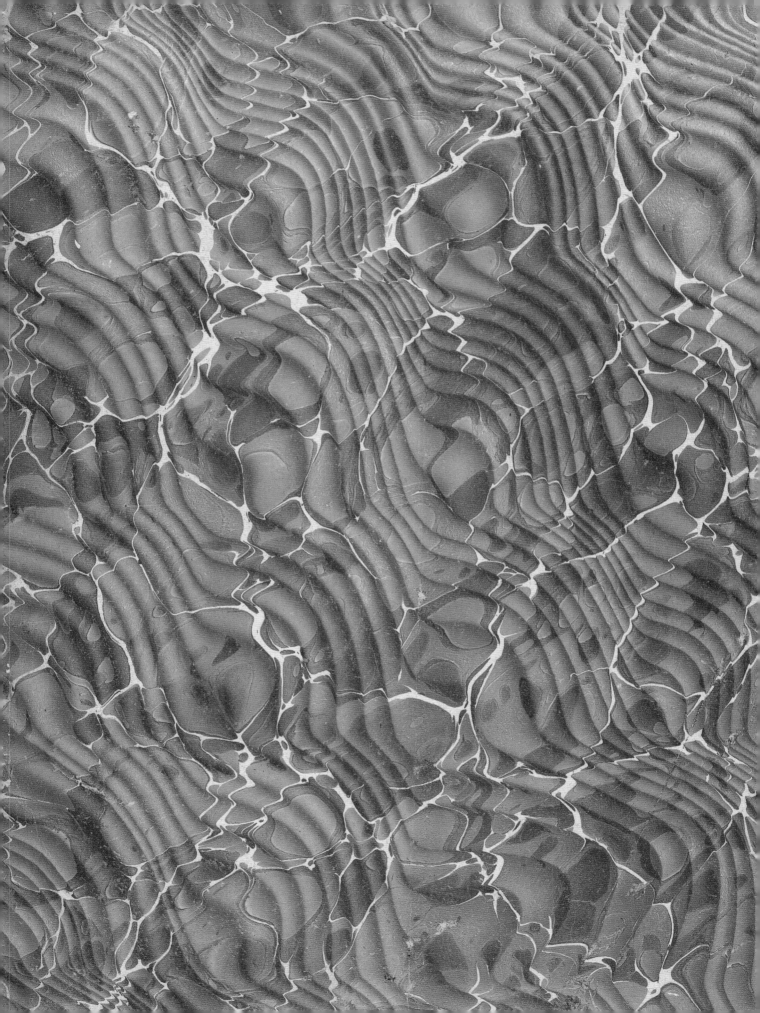

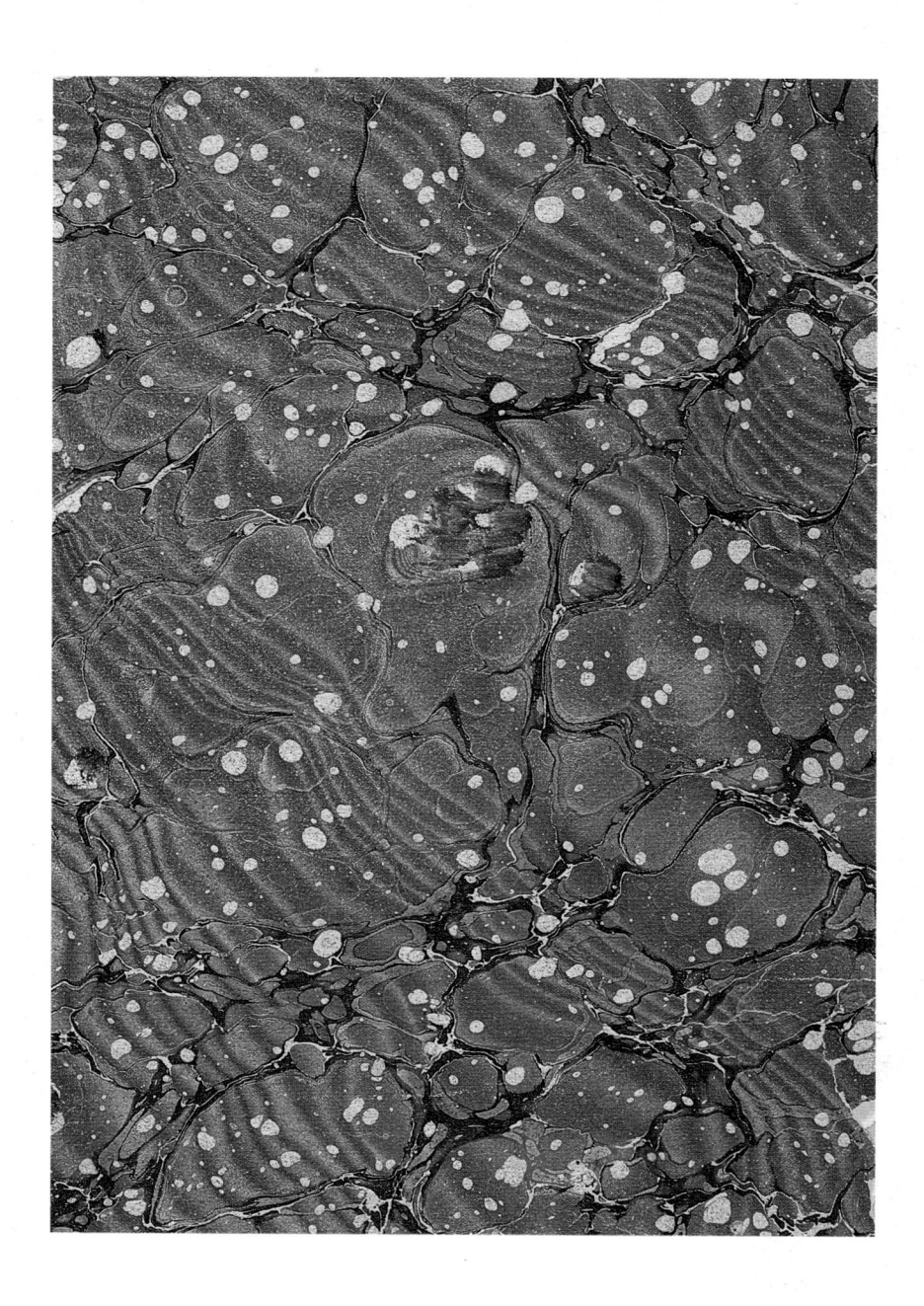

∧ The beautiful, muted earth colors of this sheet must have been composed with the eye of an artist. Note that the marbler (over a century ago) touched up the sheet with brown paint and a brush to repair a large bubble in the center. Such a technical problem is familiar to today's marblers, who solve it the same way.

══════════

< This fine example, from around 1865, shows an almost mechanically perfect SPANISH WAVE pattern. We can only guess at the techniques the artist used to create it, for most Victorian marblers left no records.

< This utterly simple
and stunning sheet was made
by one of the best modern marblers,
the late Christopher Weimann.
Christopher mastered the
traditional Turkish ways
before he began to create
his own ethereal designs.

> Christopher Weimann
created this delicate flower
as part of a series of blossoms
with a Turkish pedigree.

> Overleaf:
Fernando Machado
marbled this brilliantly
colored sheet twice.

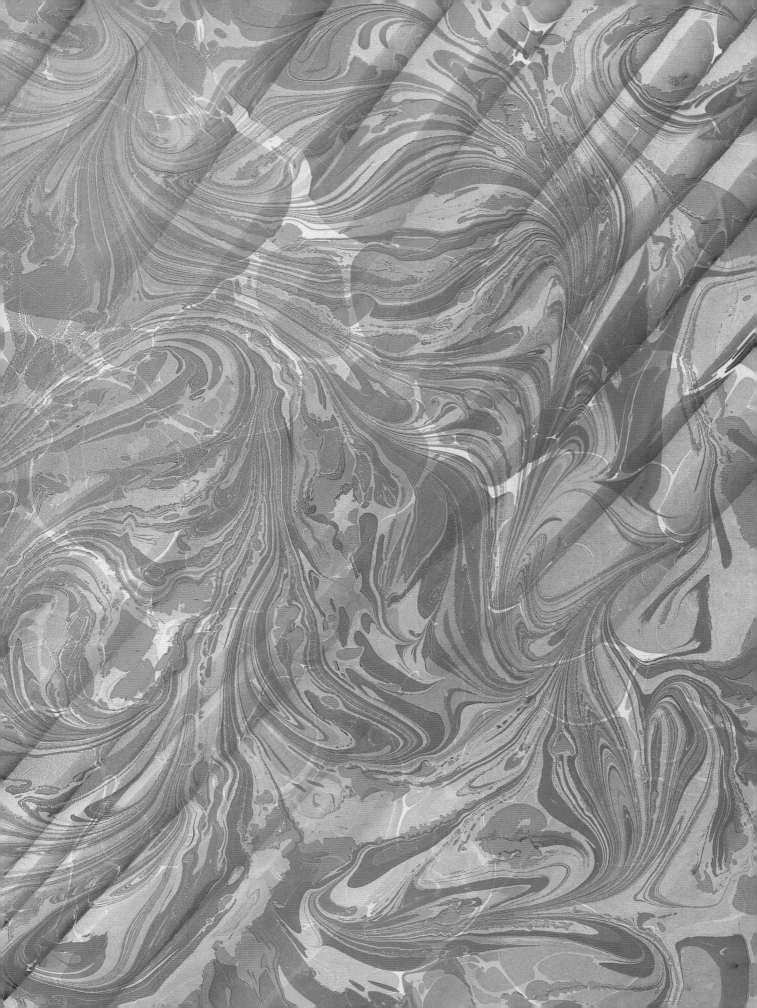

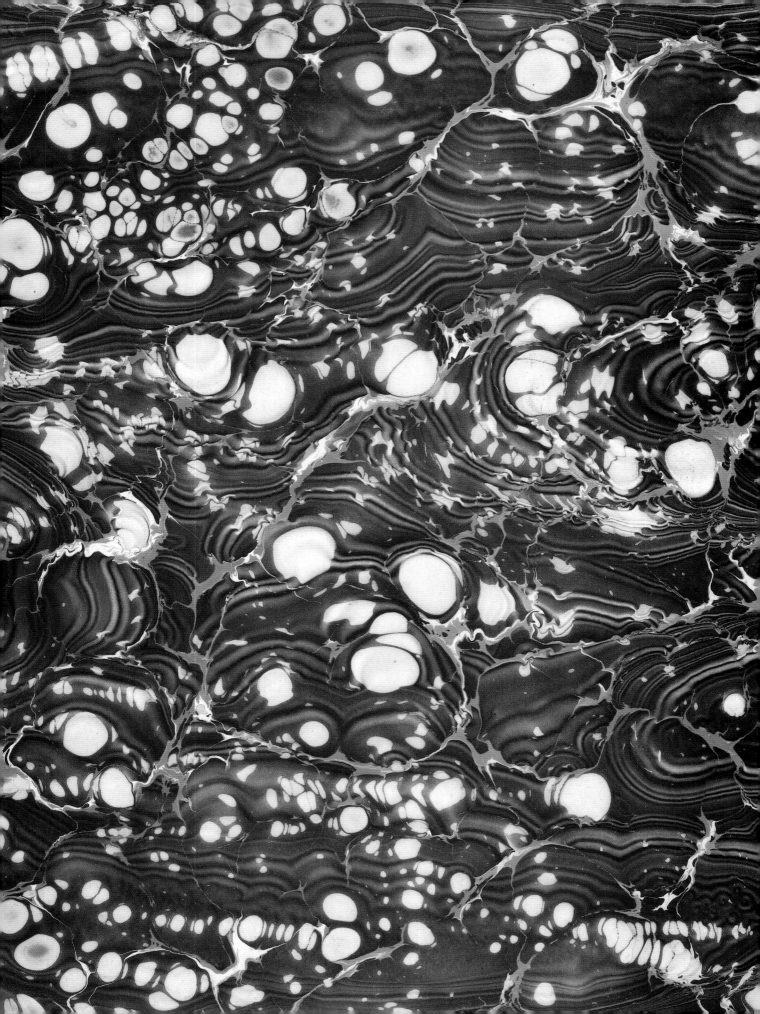

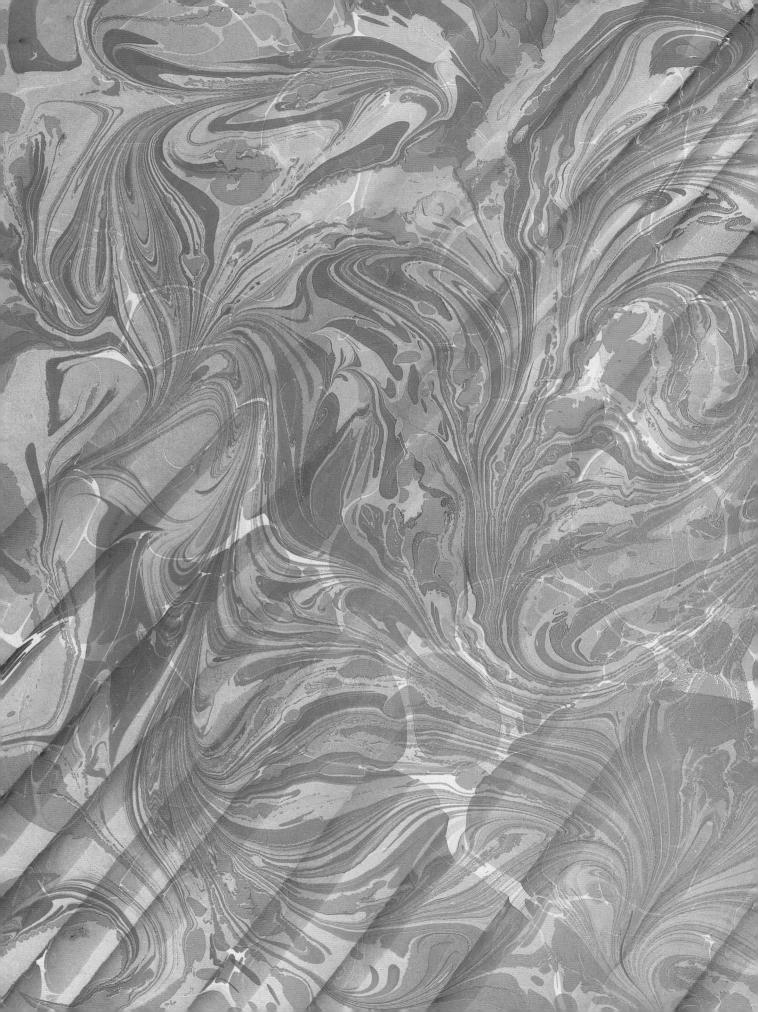

< This utterly simple
and stunning sheet was made
by one of the best modern marblers,
the late Christopher Weimann.
Christopher mastered the
traditional Turkish ways
before he began to create
his own ethereal designs.

===

> Christopher Weimann
created this delicate flower
as part of a series of blossoms
with a Turkish pedigree.

===

> Overleaf:
Fernando Machado
marbled this brilliantly
colored sheet twice.

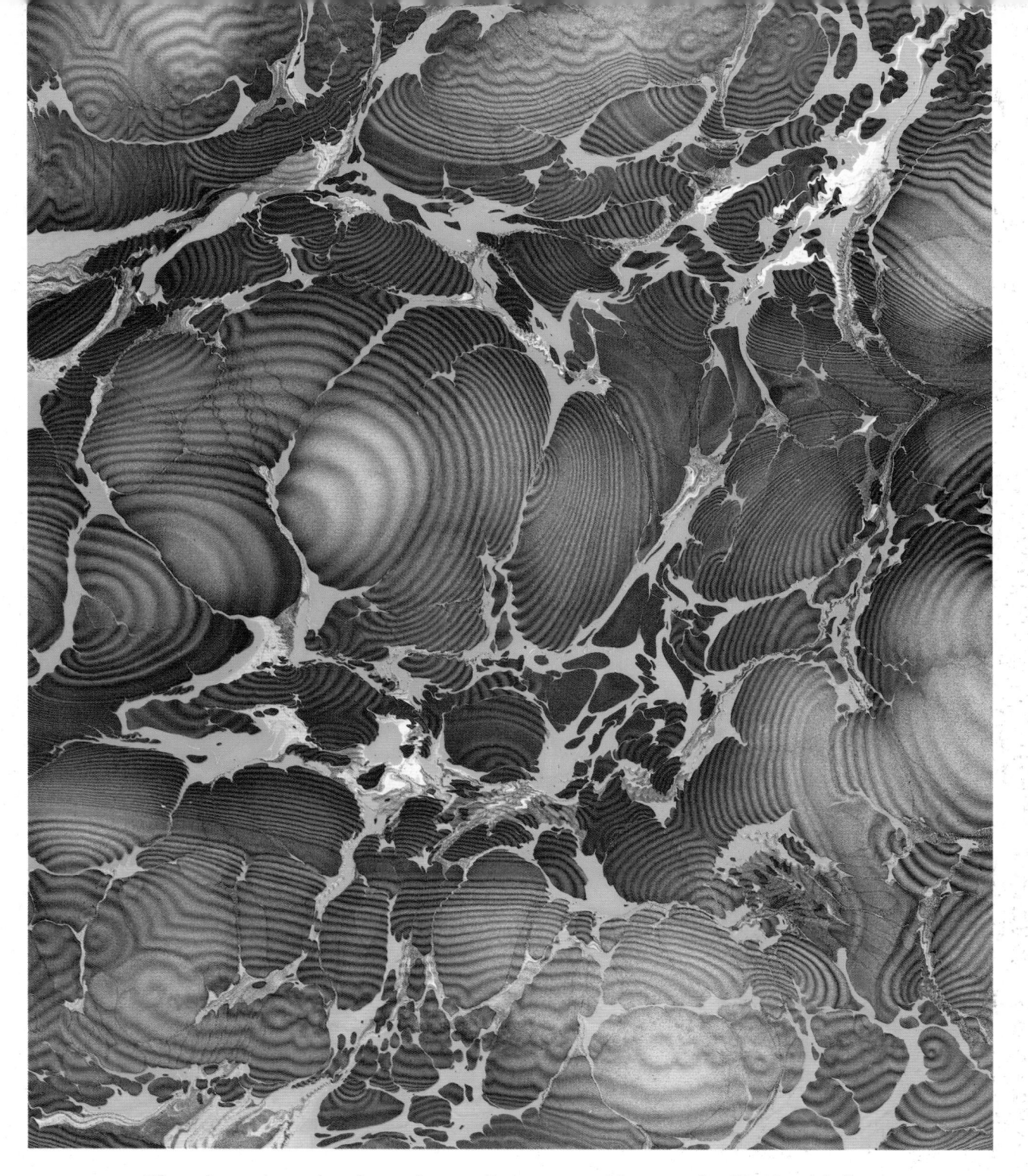

∧ These large, irregular shapes bear a distinct resemblance to fossilized seashells,
whose striations were created by shifting the paper from side to side.

< Bold use of elementary colors created this electrifying look.

> The following pages reveal the author's love of many-layered patterns.
Pages 22-23: The cloud formations were an accident; the marbler's paint became fouled with a
wax-like additive. Pages 24-25: This watery design has the endless variety of nature.

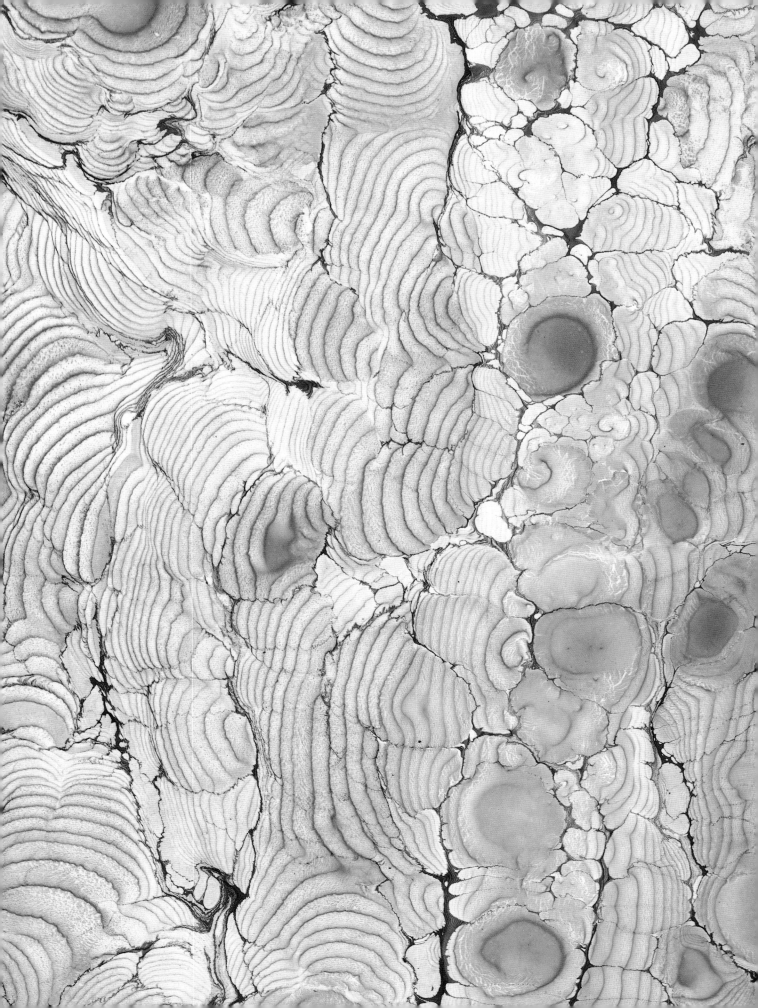

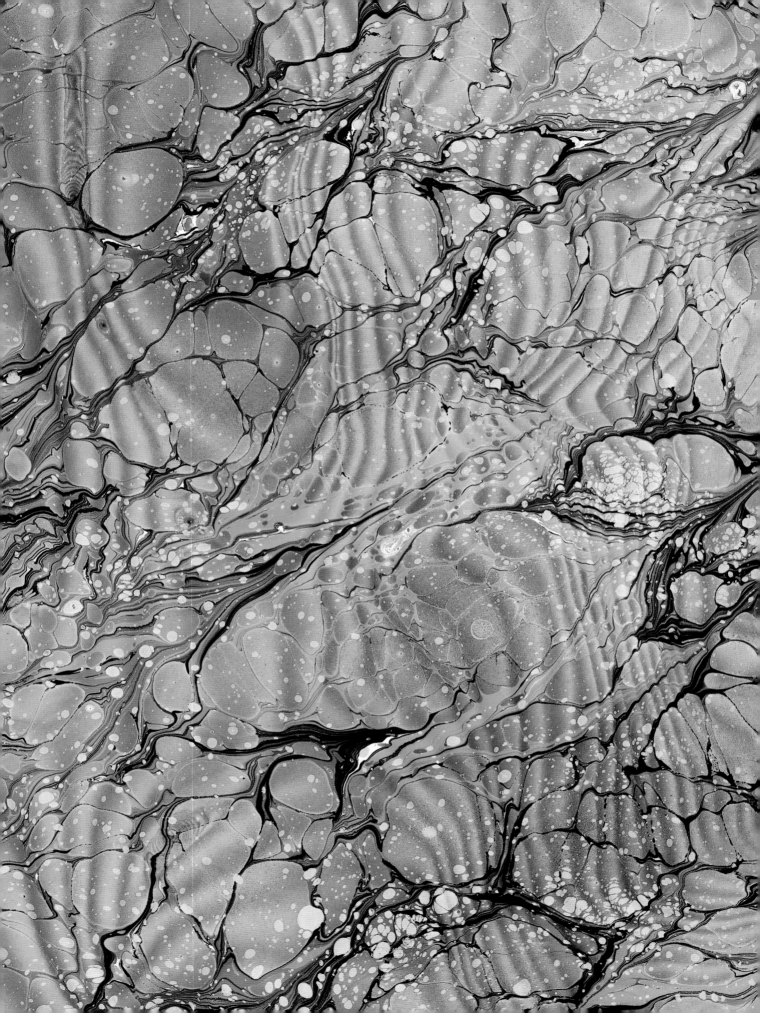

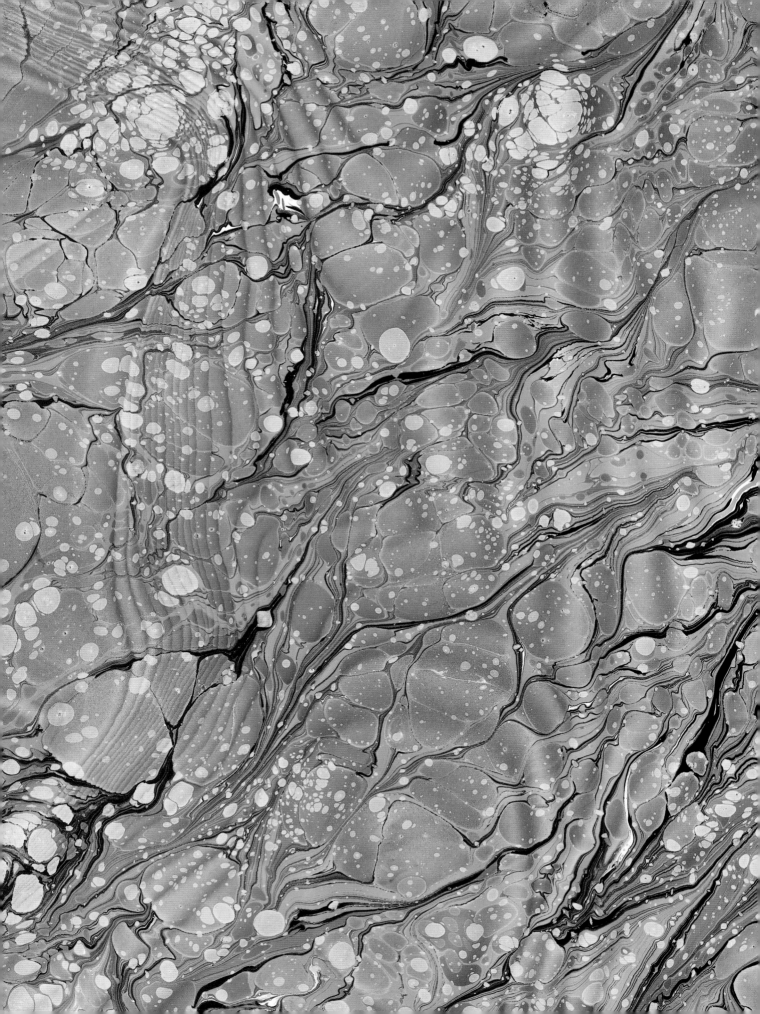

∧ Made by Julie Addison, a San Francisco marbler
for twenty-five years, this example of stencil marbling
was made by first laboriously cutting a detailed
stencil out of waterproof paper.

> This dreamy field of gold and silver was created by Julie Addison.
The delicate frost-like formations are fascinating.

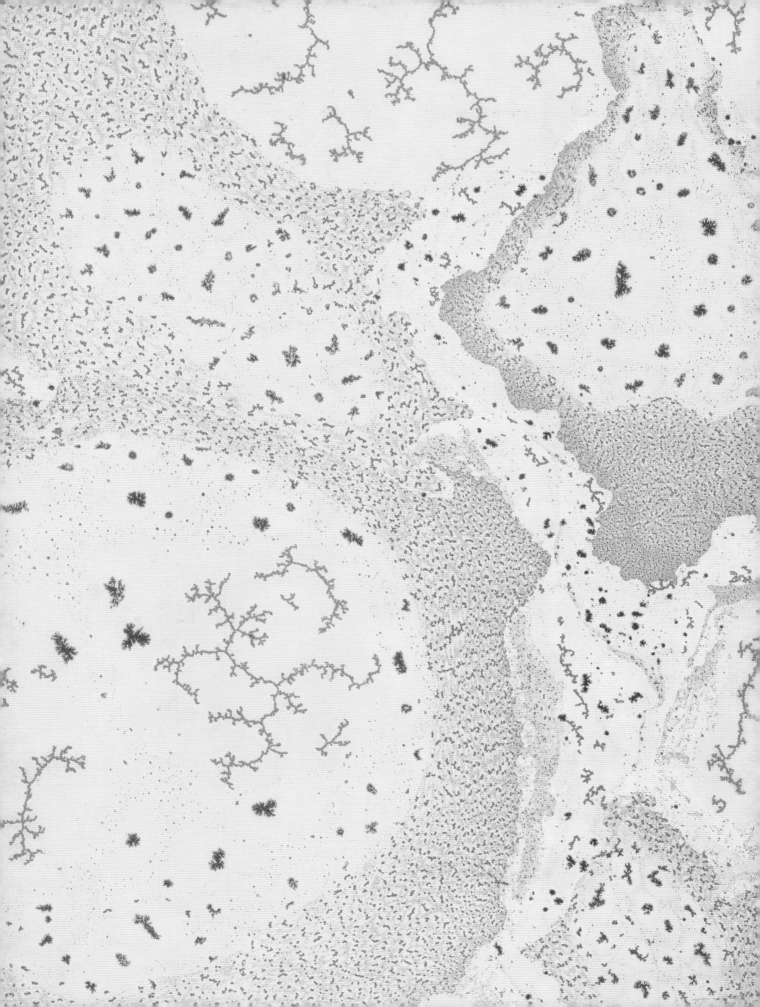

∧ At the dense and complex end of the spectrum is this double-marbled sheet.
The exuberant effect reflects its creator, who goes simply by the name of Cove.

< The papers created by "Olaf," in Berkeley, California, have a microcosmic feel.
He will throw any combination of paints onto his watery size for new effect.

> Overleaf: Olaf applied eighty droplets of paint to create this butterfly pattern,
with a tiny amount of spreading agent to open the white areas.

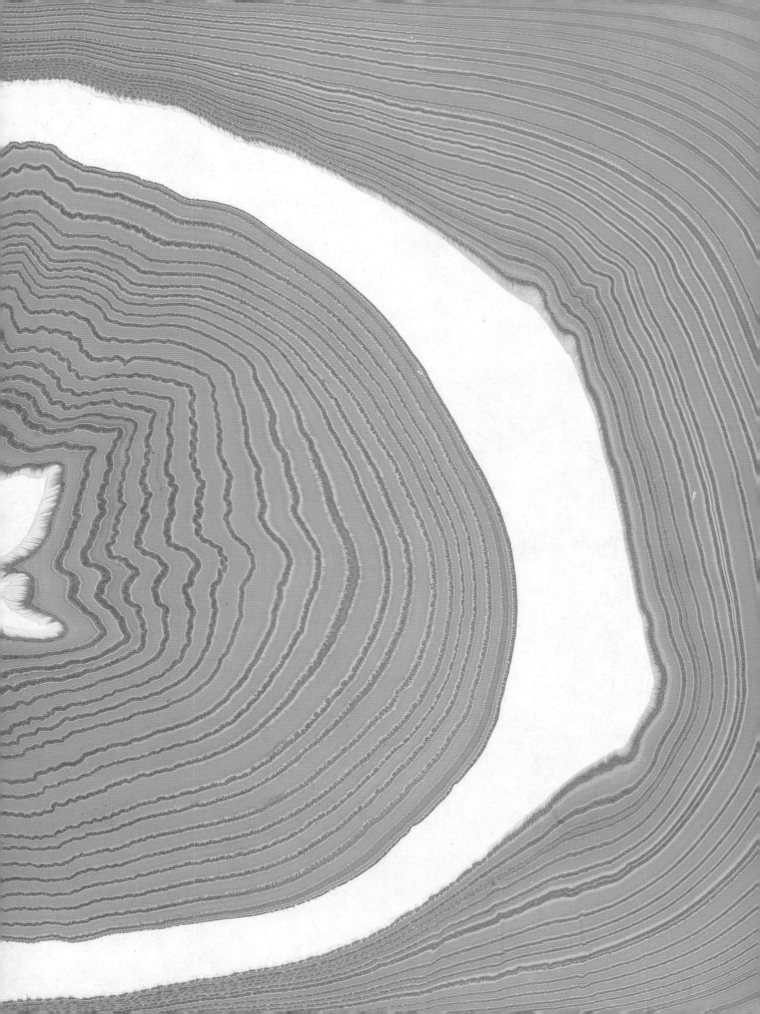

Four vignettes by the marbler Olaf, each reminiscent of a pattern in nature.

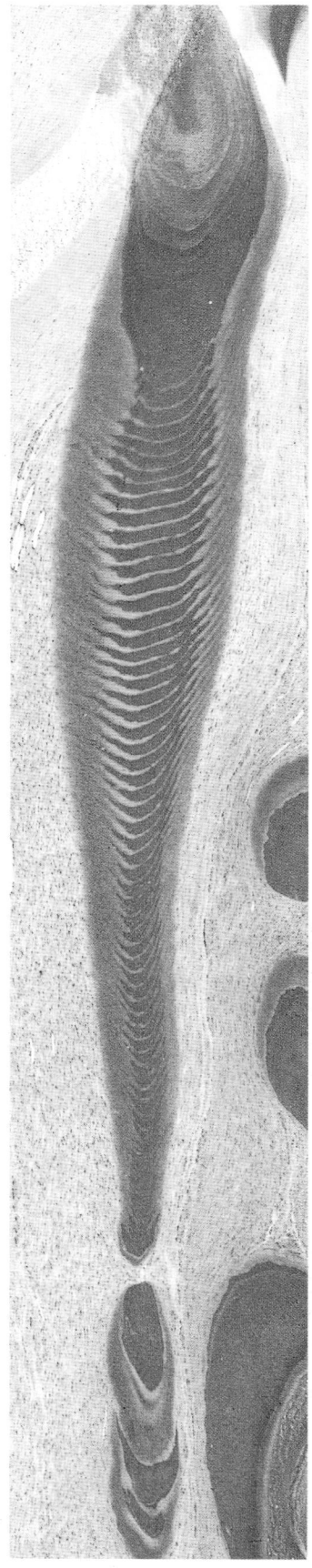

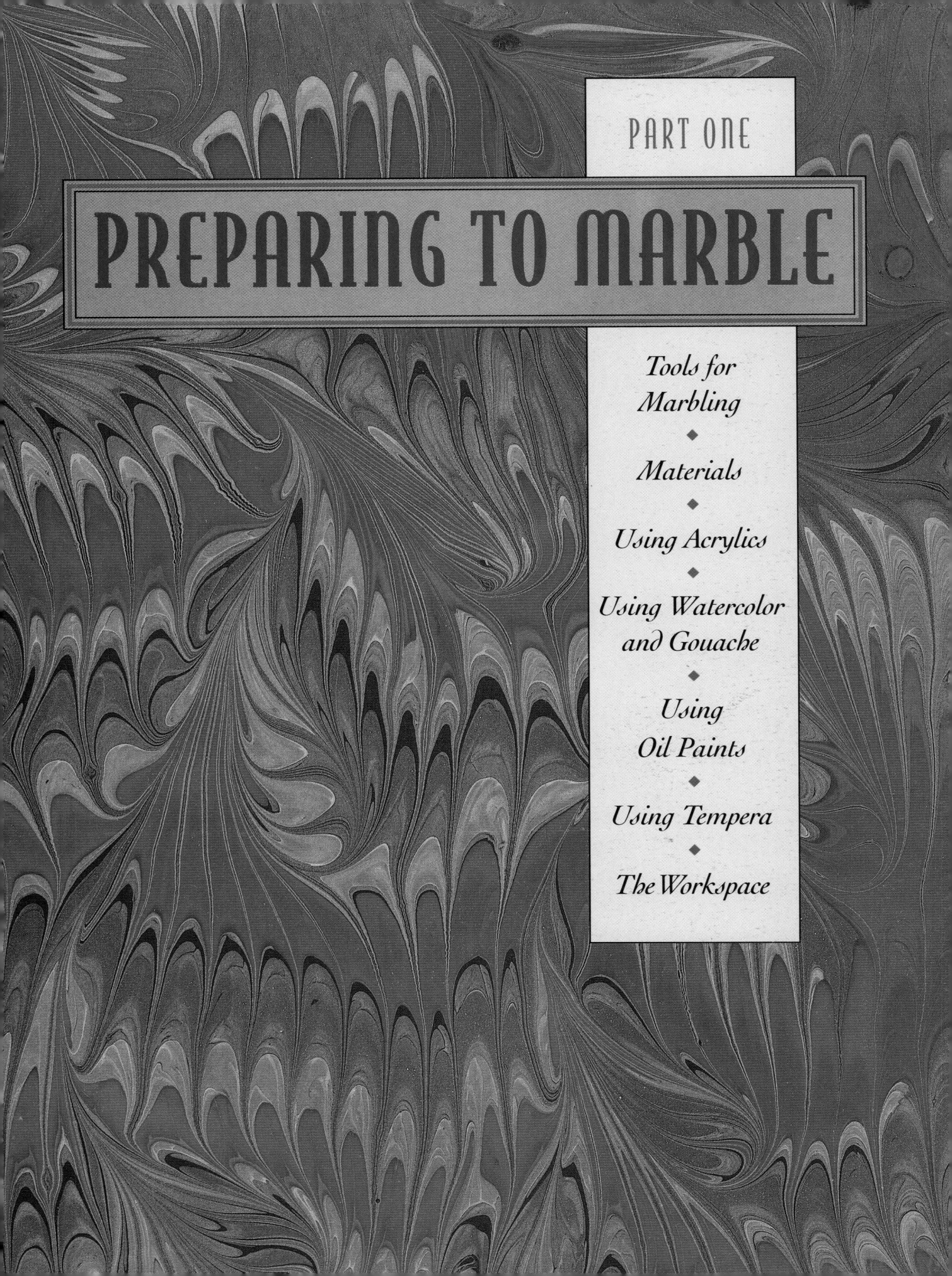

PART ONE

PREPARING TO MARBLE

Tools for
Marbling

◆

Materials

◆

Using Acrylics

◆

Using Watercolor
and Gouache

◆

Using
Oil Paints

◆

Using Tempera

◆

The Workspace

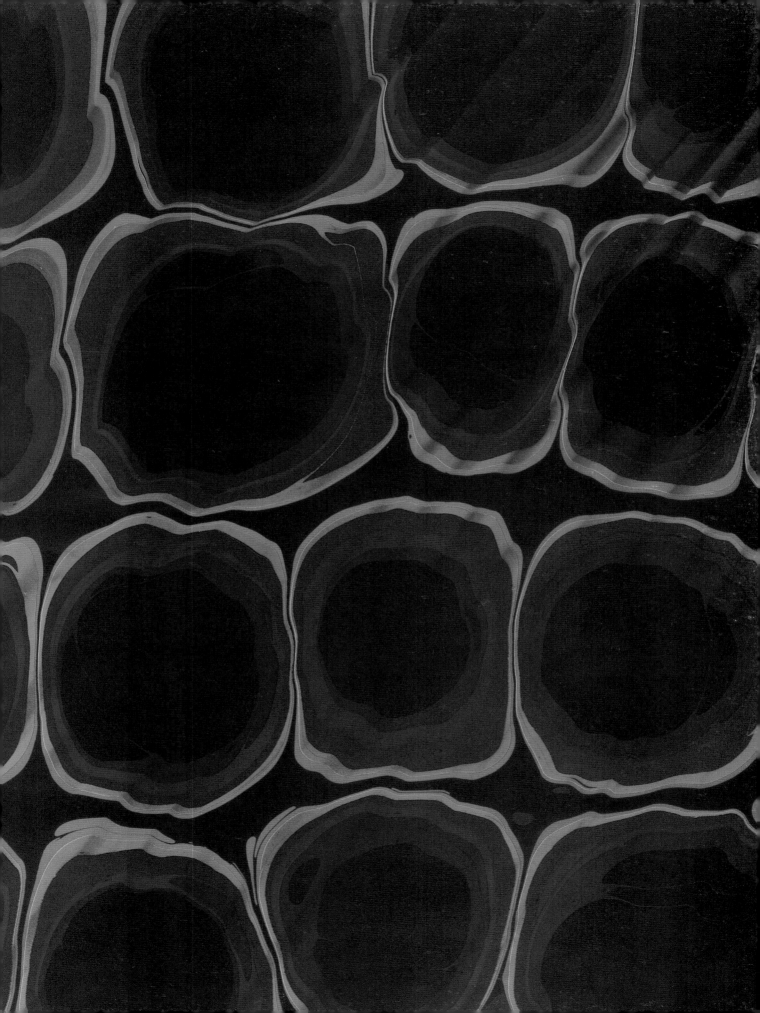

TOOLS FOR MARBLING

As you flip through catalogs of marbling-supply houses, you can find custom-made rakes and combs with solid-brass fittings for $80 or so; you can find custom-made trays with eight coats of varnish, and there are plenty of other kinds of exotic tools with big price tags. Beginning marblers should understand that any and all tools for marbling can be made by themselves for very little money, or can be found at a local hardware store or supermarket for next to nothing. There is no reason to invest a large amount of money in marbling tools. The tools you will need— a tray, a whisk, a rake, and so on—are described in the following pages, along with instructions on how to make the tool for pennies or buy it for only a few dollars more.

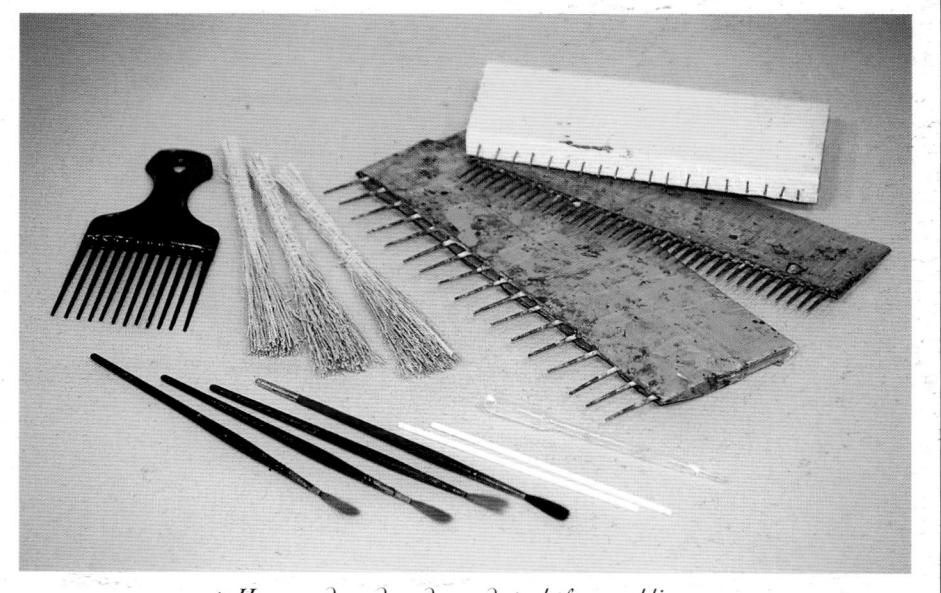

∧ *Homemade and ready-made tools for marbling.*

< *Fernando Machado used an eyedropper to create these concentric rings on black paper.*

The Tray

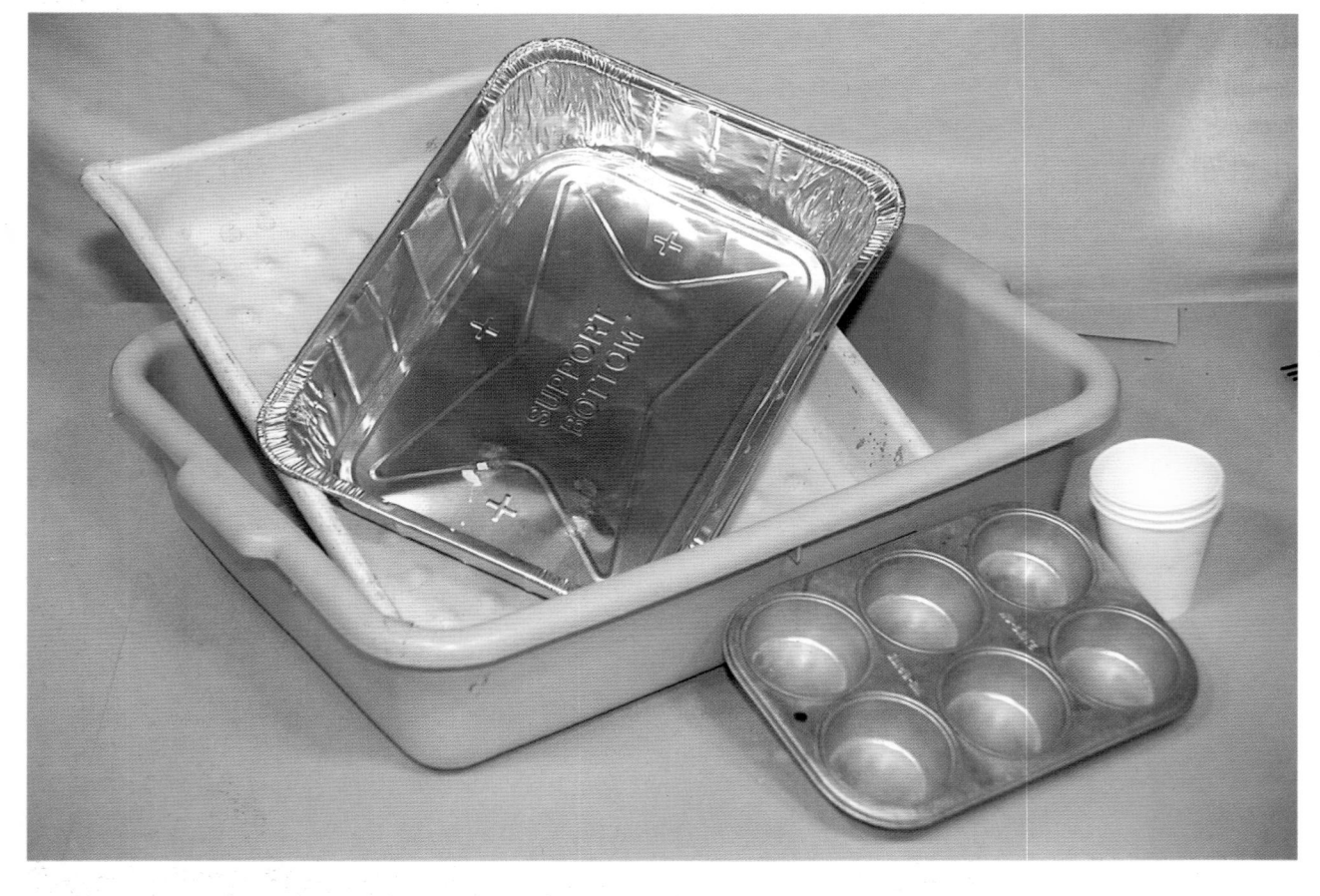

The first thing you need is a good waterproof tray to hold your marbling size. You can use many different types of containers for this. If you want to marble on paper which is 9 x 12" or smaller, a kitty-litter tray works beautifully. Also, if you are marbling smaller papers, aluminum roasting tins work very well. If you want larger sheets of paper, photo trays are available all the way up to 26 x 34"; these are slightly more expensive but will last for a very long time. Teflon-coated trays also cost more, but clean up quickly. Plastic sweater-storage boxes are also fine.

If you are fabric marbling, and you have an odd-sized piece of fabric, you can custom-make a very inexpensive tray by lining a suitable cardboard box with a sheet of plastic (see opposite page). This is a very simple type of tray that you can make for pennies, although it is just a "one-shot" tray.

Trays are easy to find in housewares and hardware stores. Muffin tins make handy paint containers.

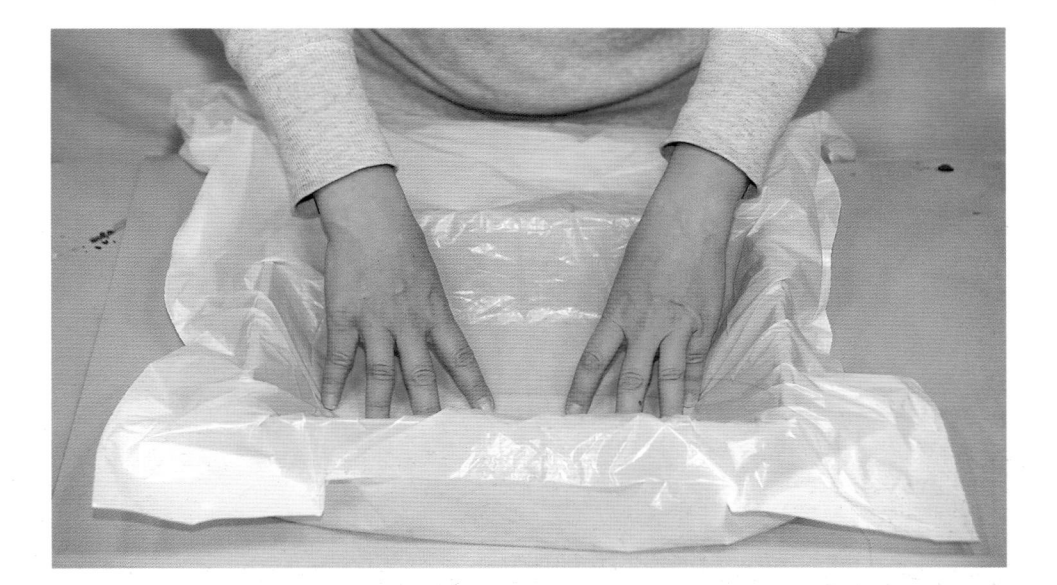

Insert your shallow cardboard box into a white plastic bag. Push the bag down into the box.

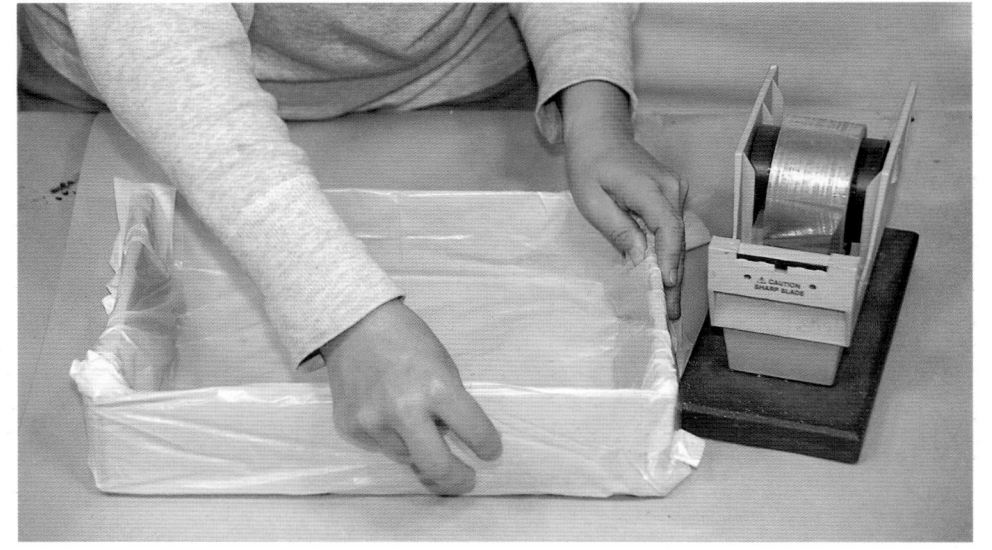

Tape around the edges secures the liner.

When you are done, simply wrap and tie up old size to discard it.

Hand Tools

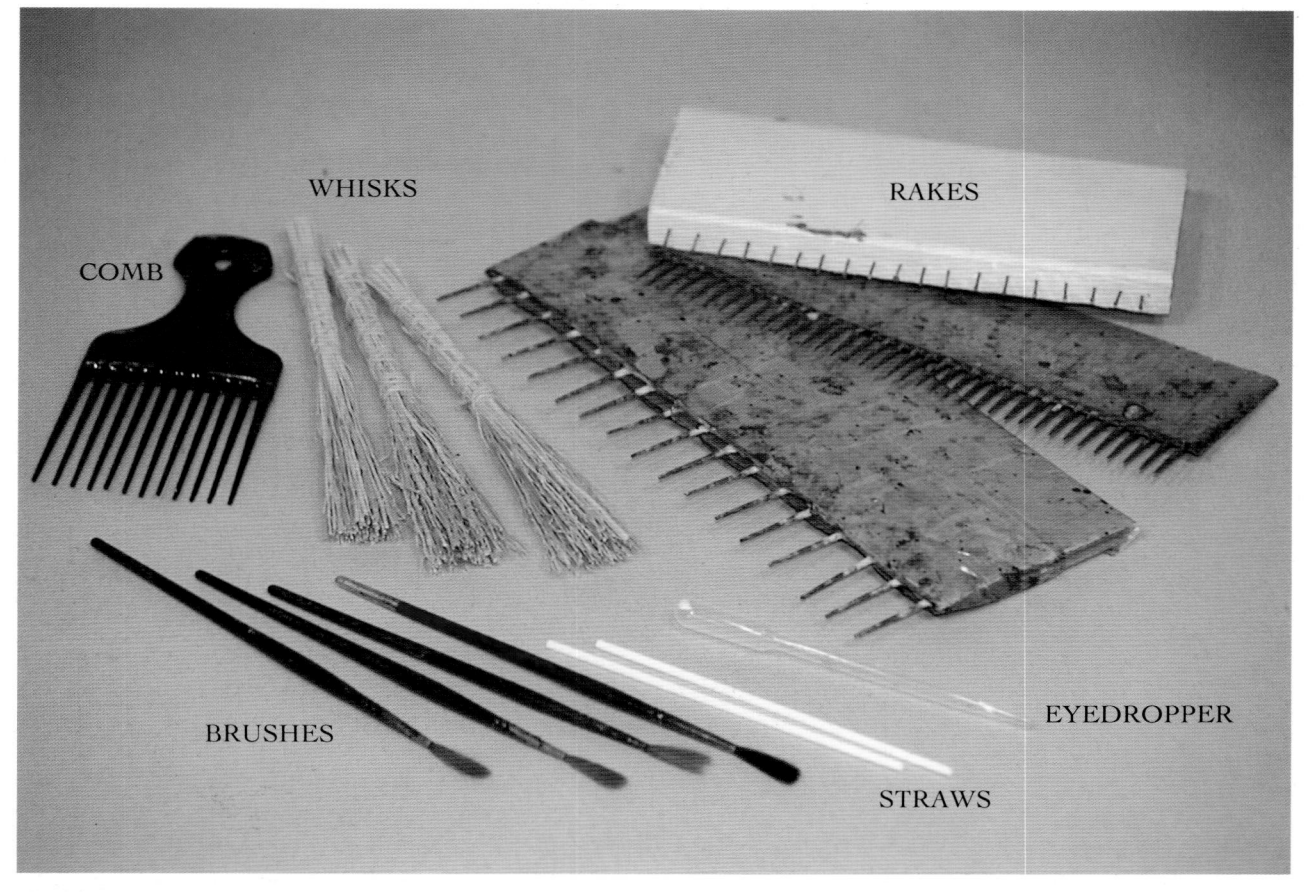

Most marbling tools are easily made of common household materials, so I urge you to think creatively and make them yourself out of whatever you have on hand.

THE WHISK OR BRUSH

One item that you absolutely must have is the traditional tool for applying the paints: a broom corn whisk, or a broom corn brush. This is a small bunch of broom corn which has been tied up at one end and is approximately 6" to 8" long. The loose and bristly stems are used to mix and stir your marbling paints and also to spatter the surface of

the size. What makes the broom corn whisk necessary and unique is that each bristle end will pick up a different-sized droplet of paint and deposit it on the surface. This is the only way to get such well-favored marbled patterns as the Turkish Stone and the Antique Spot.

You can buy broom corn whisks ready-made or make them yourself very easily by using an old broom. Simply remove the wire or string binding the broom and cut off at least a handful of the broom corn in 8" lengths. Tap it down so that the raggedy ends are all flush with each other, and then bind the top into a tight bundle to make your handle.

Cut the bristles for your whisk from broom corn at a length of at least 8".

Use filament tape, string, wire, or raffia for binding one end of the bundle.

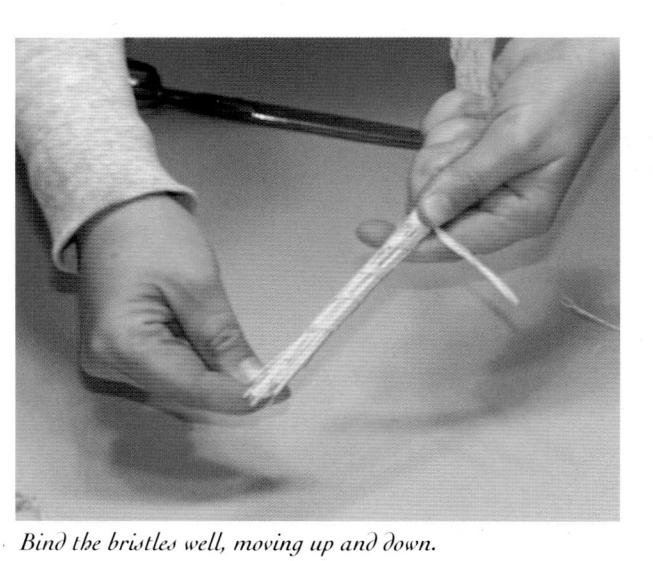

Bind the bristles well, moving up and down.

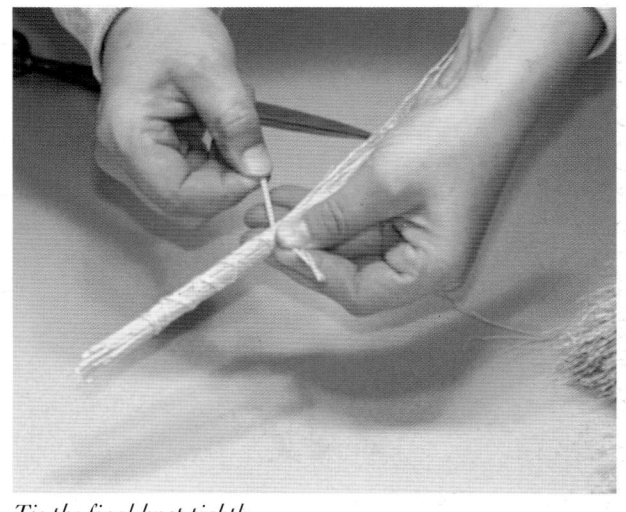

Tie the final knot tightly.

Trim both ends.

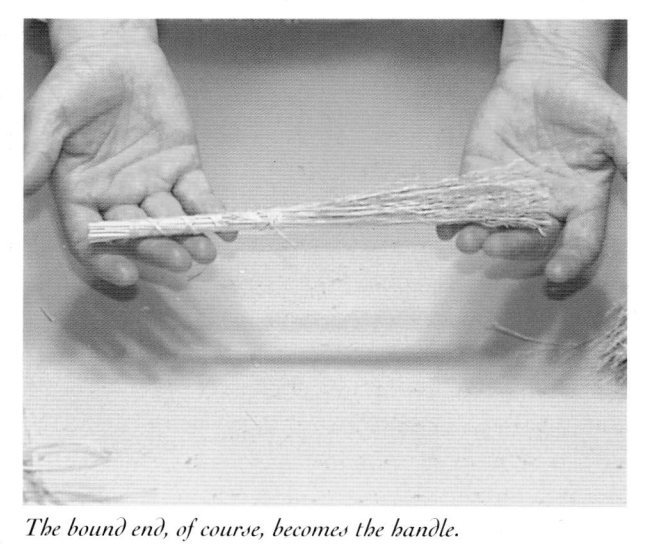

The bound end, of course, becomes the handle.

Use filament tape, string, wire, or raffia for binding and then trim both ends neatly. The broom corn brush needs to be about 3/8" thick at the handle end.

I recommend making several whisks at once. In marbling, you will want to have a separate whisk for each color.

You can also use paint brushes for applying your paints, but they create an entirely different look. They will pick up a much larger droplet of paint, and you will not get a wonderful variegated stone pattern. If you do use paint brushes, use those which have very long and droopy bristles on them. You want a brush which is somewhat limp.

SLOTTED SPOON

Another very handy tool for which you will find many uses is a slotted spoon. I find wonderful metal slotted spoons in thrift stores among the kitchen gadgets, and they work just perfectly for mixing up your size and for pulling out some of the thickened globs that could interfere with your designs.

RAKES AND COMBS

Rakes and combs can be made easily from common household materials. One method is to take toothpicks and insert them into the holes which line corrugated cardboard, as is demonstrated here. Other easy methods using household materials include gluing or taping hair picks, T-pins, or nails to a strip of cardboard the width of your marbling tray. You can also use balsa wood or foamcore board; both are very effective bases on which to attach the tines of your rake.

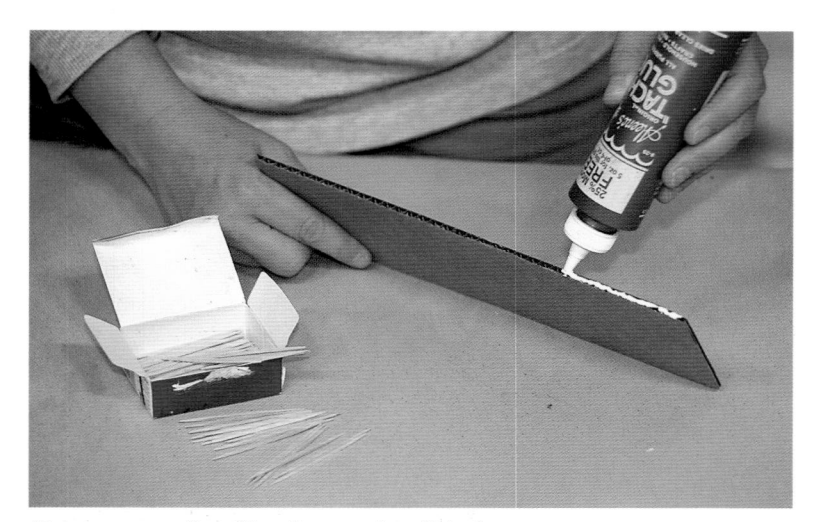

Using corrugated cardboard cut to the width of your marbling tray, put a line of glue along the edge.

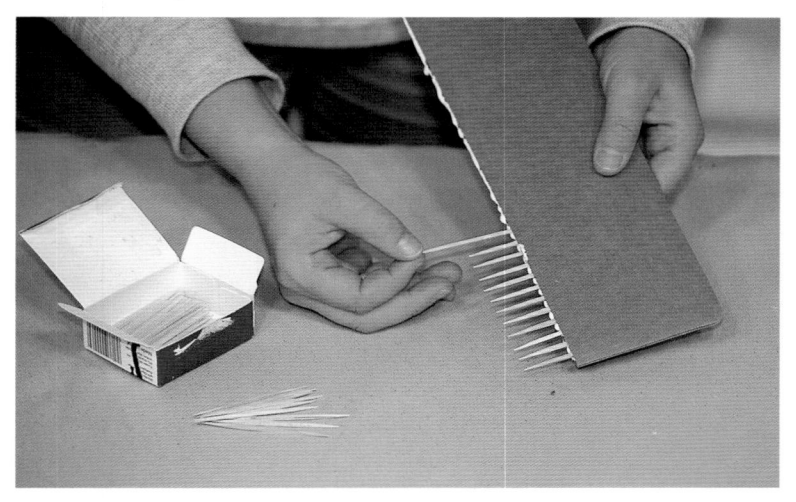

Using toothpicks for the tines of your rake, insert them in every other slot in the cardboard edge.

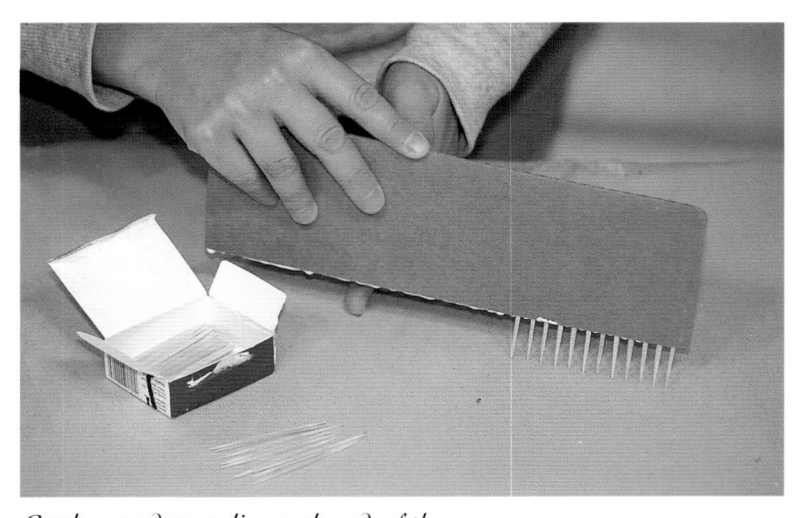

Gently press down to line up the ends of the toothpicks before the glue sets.

STYLUS AND EYEDROPPER

In order to make some of the combed patterns and the beautiful painted images, you will need a stylus and an eyedropper. A stylus can be anything ranging from a pencil to a toothpick to a straw. A very small stylus will give you a very small amount of "drag"—the action of pulling and disturbing the paint it's moving through. A larger stylus, something with about the thickness of a pencil, will give you a broad, sweeping pull.

Eyedroppers can usually be obtained at drugstores, but if you do not want to make a special trip, a plastic drinking straw will do the job. In order to use a straw as an eyedropper, dip it into your paints all the way to the bottom of the container and put your finger tightly over the mouth of the straw in order to create a vacuum. Lift up the straw, keeping your finger on the top, and touch it down briefly onto the surface of the size, at the same time letting up on just the barest amount of the pressure from your finger on the mouth of the straw. This will release one drop of paint onto the surface of your size.

PAINT CONTAINERS

You will need to take a little extra care in securing paint-mixing cups. Paper cups sometimes do not work, for many have been treated with a wax-like material to make them nonabsorbent to liquids. Sometimes the wax materials can be dissolved into your paint, destroying its workability. I recommend using clean glass jars; baby-food jars are ideal, because you can cap them afterwards and keep your leftover paints. Most mixed marbling paints can be kept a few weeks, although they may need to be readjusted before use, since some evaporation and settling will have occured.

A wonderful item to have on hand for marbling with children is muffin tins. You can mix up an array of colors, but the best thing about them is that the paints are unlikely to get tipped over.

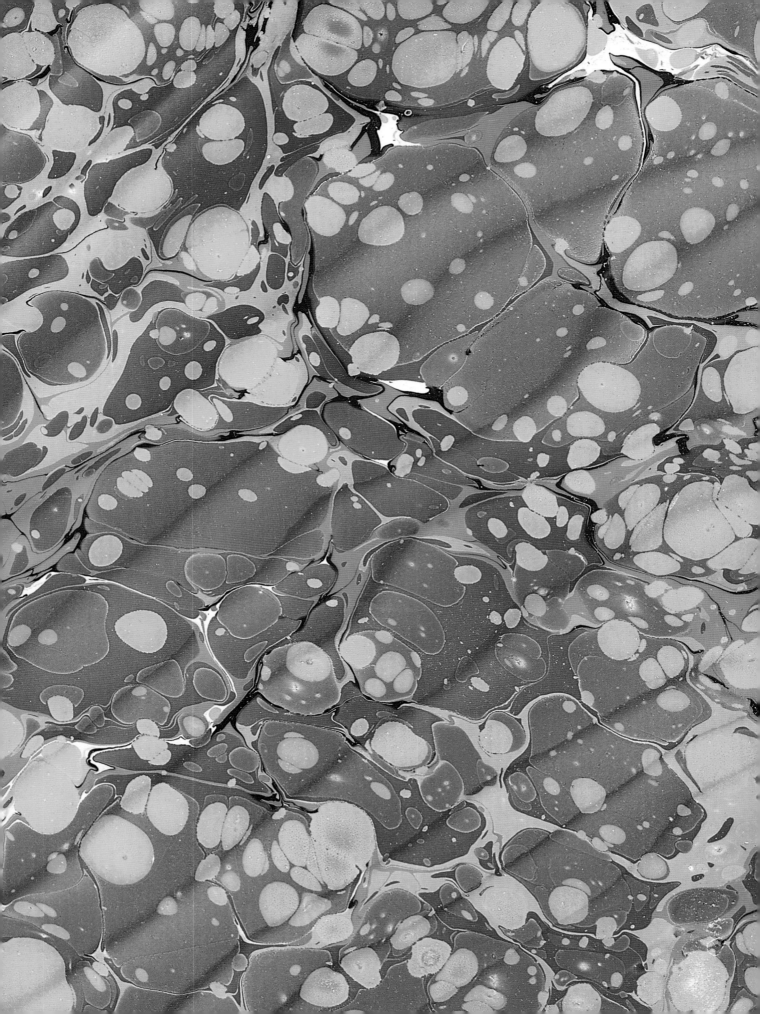

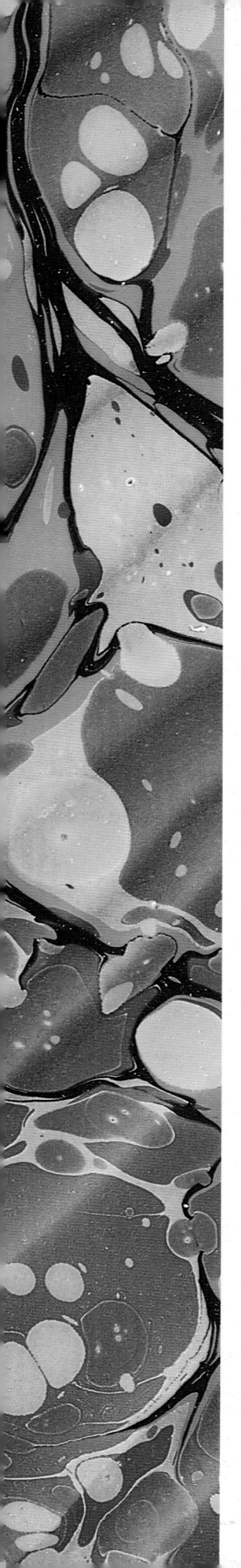

MATERIALS

arbling may seem complex, but it is not. It has always involved the patterning of paints floating on a thickened water base. There is no one proper way to make this magic happen, contrary to the more esoteric manuals available. Marbling has been constantly changing since its inception. And though some sources of instruction aim at "traditional marbling," there is really no such thing. In the following pages we'll see that while the materials for marbling are immensely varied, there are three basic types of materials necessary: Size, paper, and paints.

∧ *Paints floating on size are instantly transferred to paper.*

< *Opaque watercolor, or gouache, was used here.*

The Size

Thickened water (size) will support the paints.

The first of the basic materials you need is called the *size*, or the size base. This is a "thickened water" which will be about 2" to 3" deep sitting in a waterproof tray. This liquid will act as the supportive base for the paint which will float on its highly slippery surface.

One of the obvious points that you need to remember is that, since the purpose of the size base is to support the paint, it must be considerably thicker than your paint. I recommend that your size be at least the thickness of buttermilk. Take care not to create a size which is pudding-like, for this will inhibit the spreading of your paints.

The three most common size materials in use today are *methocel*, a thickening agent used in the food and drug industries, *carragheen*, a seaweed derivative, and *cornstarch*. The specific size you will use will depend upon the paint you select, and I have accordingly included the different recipes for size with the discussions of the paints they are best suited for.

Any size you use may have a coating of bubbles on top, which you must remove by laying onto the surface a sheet of newspaper the size of your tray. After about two seconds, lift it up and throw it away. You need to repeat this until most of the bubbles floating on the surface are gone. After that, you will need to take a strip of cardboard that is as wide as your tray and insert it into the size about 1/4" and, pulling toward you, skim off all the remaining bubbles. When they are pushed to the very edge, you may scoop them up and throw the cardboard strip into the trash.

All the marbling sizes mentioned in this book are nontoxic; however, you should never pour any of them into your plumbing—either toilet or sink—for they may thicken and plug your pipes. Never throw the size material outside anywhere, as it is extremely slippery and will remain so for quite a while. To dispose of used size, pour it into a plastic bag, tie it together, and put it into the trash can.

Before marbling, the surface of the size should be cleaned. Start by putting newsprint onto the surface.

Lift the newsprint, peeling away the bubbles on the surface of the size.

Scrape the remainder off with cardboard.

Paper

The array of papers suitable for marbling will excite your imagination.

The second basic material that you need is paper. As with the paint, there are many options open to the marbler. Almost any paper that has any absorbancy to it will work well as a marbling paper.

For obtaining the finest effects, I recommend using 100-percent rag or partially rag content papers. For a truly wonderful marbling surface, try Lanaquarelle's Laid Finish paper, from France. It has a fine tooth and will give you exquisite line quality.

The only papers that you absolutely cannot use are papers which have been plastic-coated, or which have been internally sized with a sizing medium to make them good for water color paint. Plastic coated papers and water color papers are sealed against water absorption and thus will not hold your marbling paint.

PAPER AND MORDANT

Some papers used by marblers, especially smooth-surfaced bond and cover papers, will need to be treated with a *mordant*. A mordant acts as a chemical bonding agent to attach the pigments firmly to the paper fibers.

However, with acrylic marbling you may wish to experiment without a mordant. Papers with a pronounced tooth, such as Lanaquarelle, newsprint, construction and manila papers, and hand-made papers may work fine. You just need to rinse such papers very gently once you have marbled them.

It's wise to make some test runs with your materials. Any time you notice that a lot of your paint is lost in the rinsing, you'll need to start treating your papers with a mordant such as aluminum sulphate, or alum. This material looks something

Colored cover stock, such as Mi-Tientes paper, usually needs to be treated with a mordant.

Both sides of the paper should be treated with your alum solution.

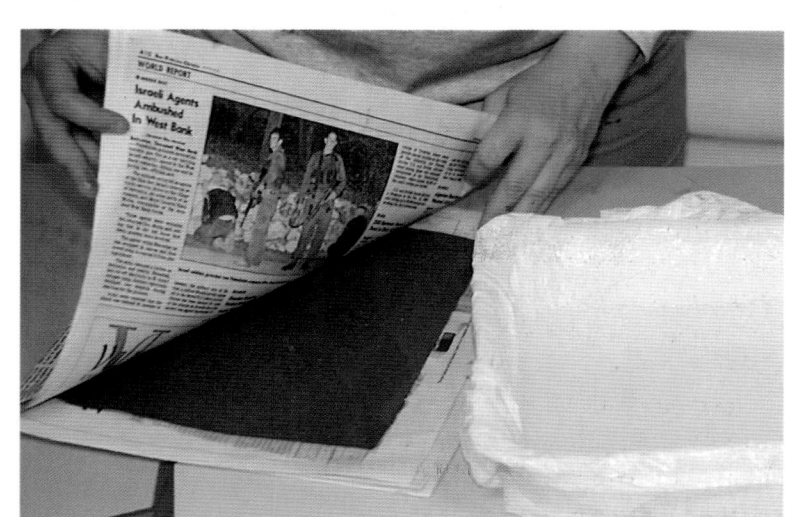

Leave to dry between newspapers for at least an hour.

like salt, and once it is dissolved, your water will be clear. Alum is not very difficult to find, for it is used in pickling. Look for it in grocery stores and in small laboratory- and chemical-supply houses.

If you are using paper which must be treated with a mordant, I recommend that you do so at least two hours before you marble, so that your papers may become reasonably dry before you begin.

After it is mixed, pour your alum solution into a tray which is the size of your marbling paper. There should be enough solution to be at least an inch deep. If you have a very large tray, you may need to make two or more batches of alum solution.

TREATING PAPER WITH MORDANT

Completely immerse your marbling paper in the alum solution. Swish it around for a few seconds. Draw the paper out, let it drip for a second or two, and then transfer it to your drying station. You may let it drip dry, which would take about two hours, or, if you are in a hurry, you may sandwich each sheet between newspapers.

The newspaper will absorb much of the alum solution and the papers will dry somewhat faster. You must remember that your alum-treated papers must be almost completely dry before you marble. If you can feel distinctly damp patches on your paper, you may notice that your paints slide right off in the rinsing process. If your papers are wrinkled when dry, you can iron them flat with an iron.

There will be times when you want to marble other surfaces than paper—a wooden box, for example, or even an egg. You should start by priming these surfaces with an acrylic *gesso*, which is available at any art-supply store.

IRONING WRINKLED PAPER

There is a final step which you may want to prepare for: ironing. After your marbled sheets have hung on the drying rack for several hours and become completely dry to the touch, you will notice that they are quite wrinkly and curled. This may make the finished papers somewhat difficult to work with, but the problem can be easily remedied by ironing your finished papers with an iron. You will need to set your iron on a medium heat setting (which is approximately the setting for cotton), and iron them on the reverse side. Do this on a surface which has some sort of padding on it; this will prevent you from ripping the sheet. This last step will result in completely flat finished pieces which can be easily mounted on boards for bookbinding or box making.

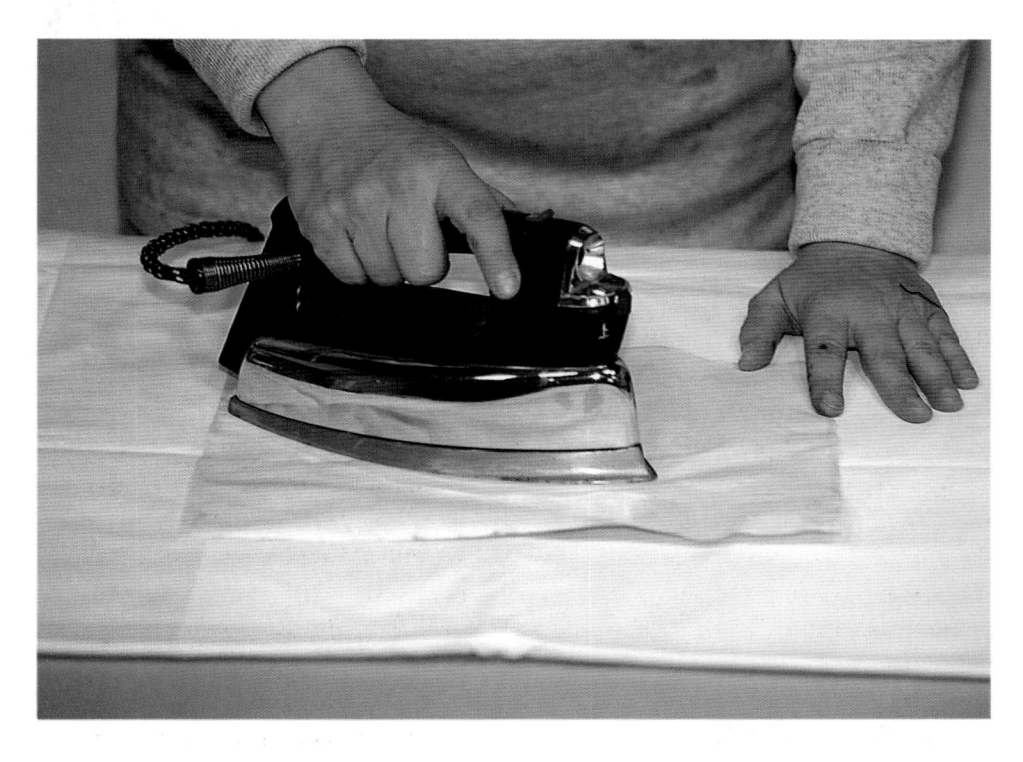

When flattening the sheet with an iron, do it on a padded surface.

The Paints

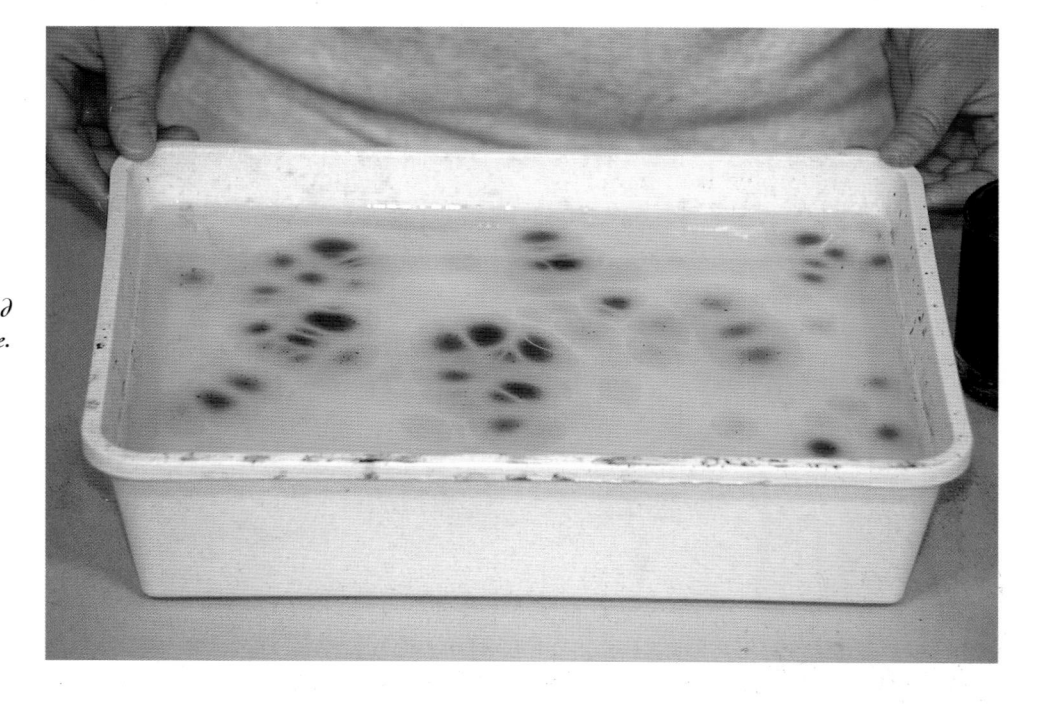

Paints should float and spread on the surface.

The third category of materials is paint. Your paints can be acrylics, tempera, gouache, printing inks, or oil paints. Some of them can be used straight from the jar and others must be thinned with water or turpentine. Many of them will need a little bit more in the way of an additive—something that will guarantee that they will spread on the top of the watery surface, and not just float. This is essential to create a beautiful film of paint with which to create your design.

SPREADING AGENTS

The way you mix your paints will determine how well and how quickly they spread or disperse on the surface of the size. Most paints (other than the Portfolio brand) will need to be mixed with a spreading agent such as ox gall (for gouache), acrylic flow medium (for acrylics), or turpentine (for oils). The spreading agent works against the surface tension of the size, which tends to keep the paint in little blobs. A sort of push-pull situation must be created. If you have an extremely thick size, you will need to add lots of spreading agent to your paints to counteract that. If you have a thin and watery size you may have to add little or no spreading agent.

Most marbling paints are pigmented paints. Each color is made with a different mineral or chemical, and each one has a different weight. Some colors are so dense and so heavy that they need a lot of spreading agent just to keep them afloat. Yet some are very light in weight, and almost seem to spread by themselves. Moreover, each color needs to be tested and adjusted separately to work with each tray size and to work with your other colors as well.

There are several things that can interfere with the spreading action of your paints. These are detailed on page 98, under "Size and Paint Problems."

COLOR MIXING

Mixing marbling colors can be tricky, for what appears in your paint cup is entirely different from what will appear on the sheet. When you drop paint onto the surface of the size, it becomes an extremely thin and sheer version of what is in your cup. Colors which appear dull or dark in your cup will bloom into brilliance once applied to the size. Colors which are used straight from the tube or jar— usually primary colors which have not been mixed with each other and are not toned down—may appear extraordinarily brilliant, even unpleasantly garish. Children sometimes prefer this look, but if you would like something subtler, you will need to tone your colors down.

Keep the following formula in mind while you are mixing: Use two parts of your primary color to one part black, and also add one part of the complementary color (which is the opposite color on the color wheel). For instance, if you are after a deep rich red, you will want to mix two parts red, one part black, and one part green. If you want subtle earthy and antique colors, you may need to add even more black and complementary tones.

A delicate, pastel look is very simply achieved by spattering about one-third to one-half the amount of paint that you normally would. In other words, simply cut down considerably on your paint usage and

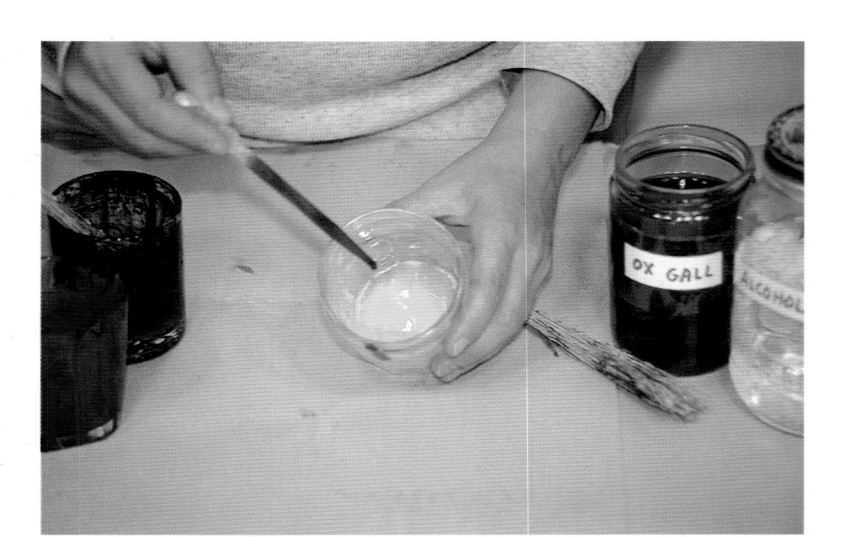

Some paints will need an additive.

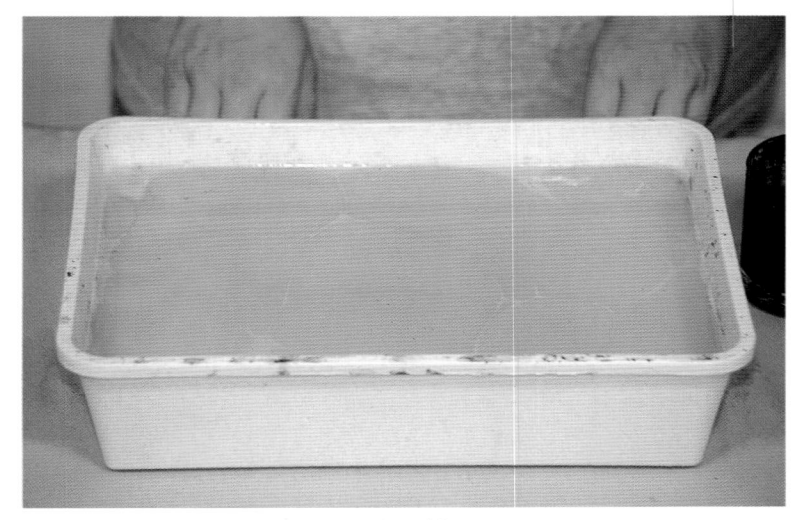

Your first color will appear to be a sheer film.

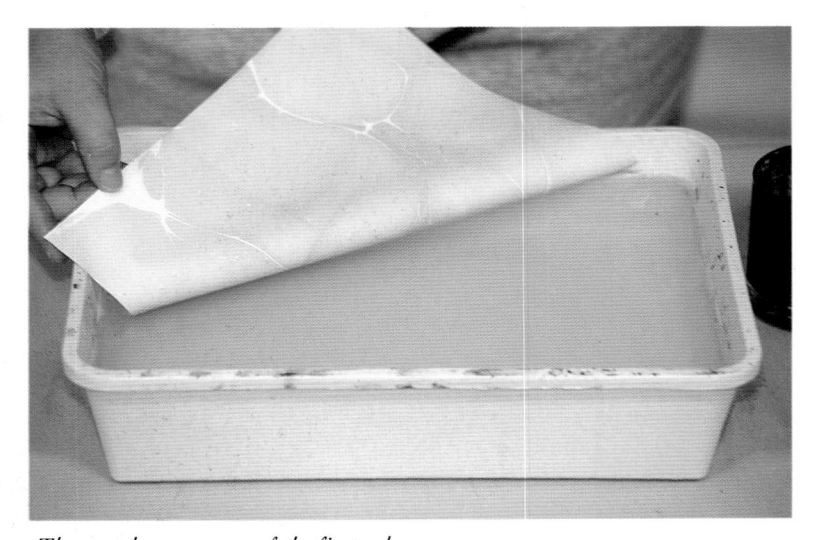

The pastel appearance of the first color.

Colors you add after that will force the first color into a veined appearance.

On the color wheel, the colors of the spectrum are arranged so that complementary colors are directly opposite each other. The complementaries blue and orange, red and green, and yellow and violet are the most familiar opposites.

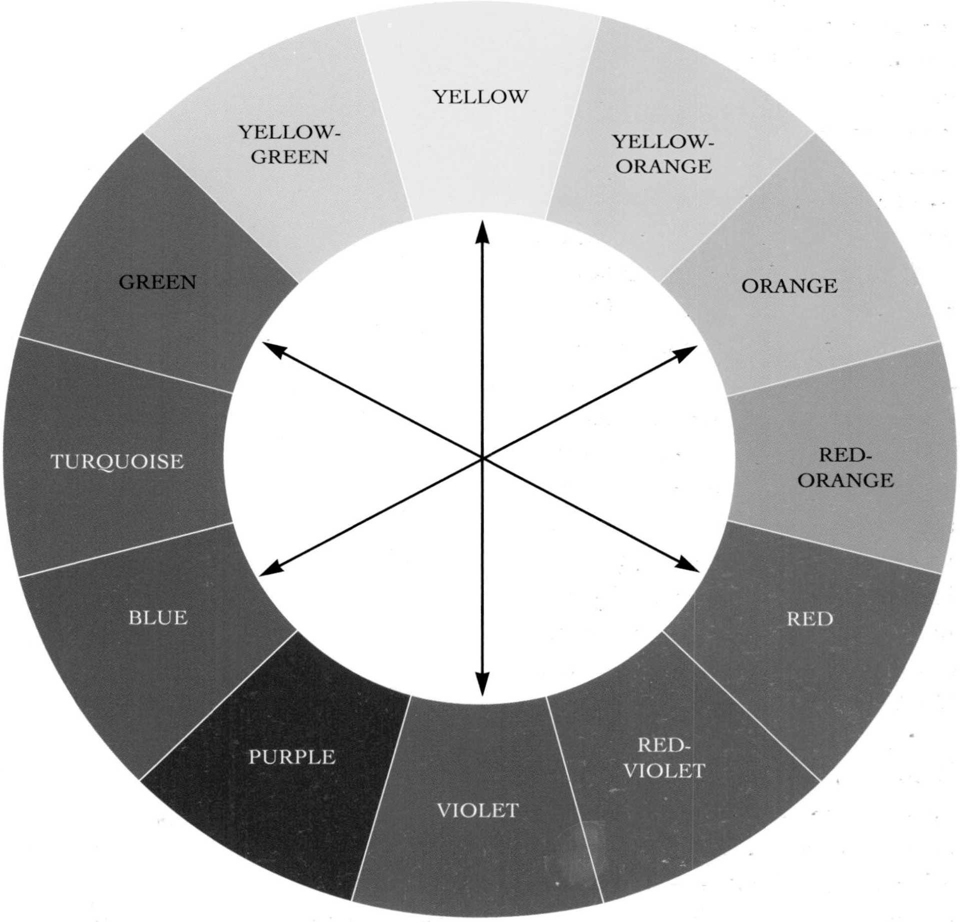

YELLOW

YELLOW-GREEN

YELLOW-ORANGE

GREEN

ORANGE

TURQUOISE

RED-ORANGE

BLUE

RED

PURPLE

RED-VIOLET

VIOLET

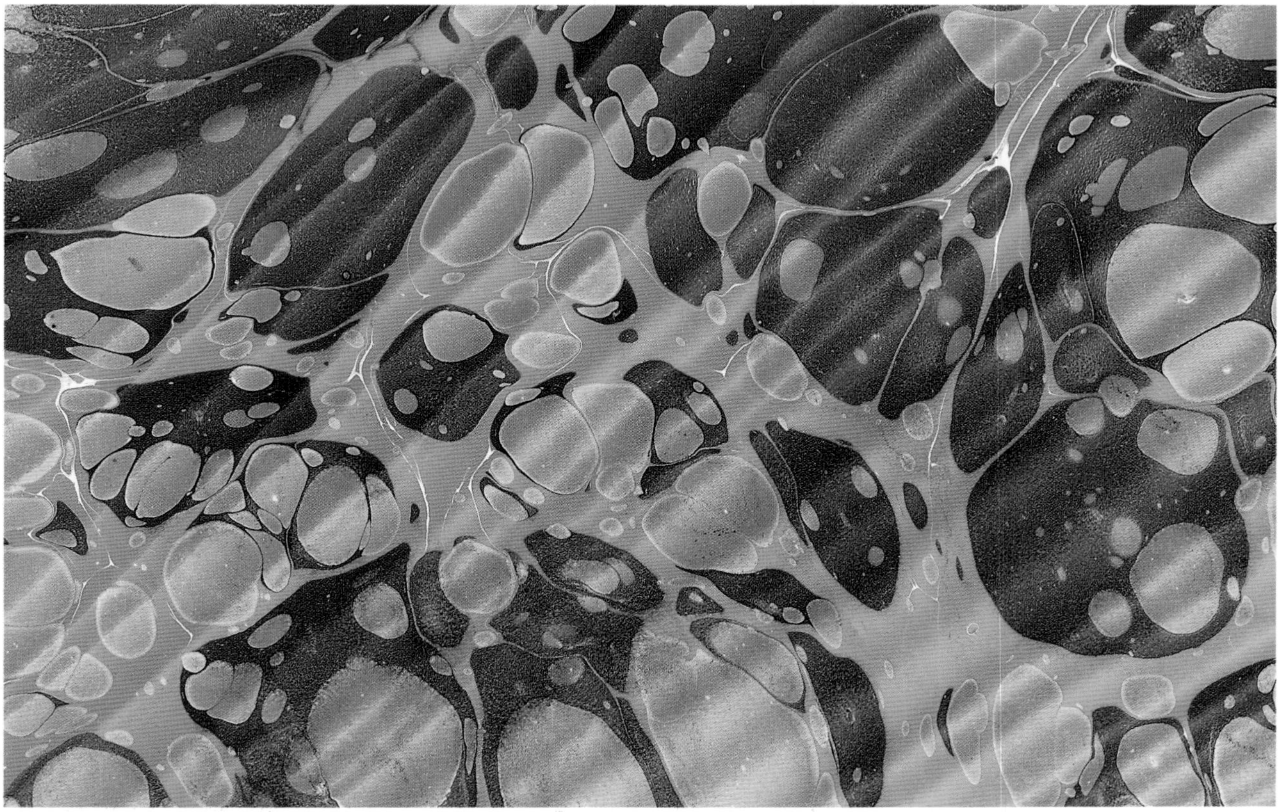

Intermixing complementary colors (colors that are opposites on the color wheel) will give you an antique look.

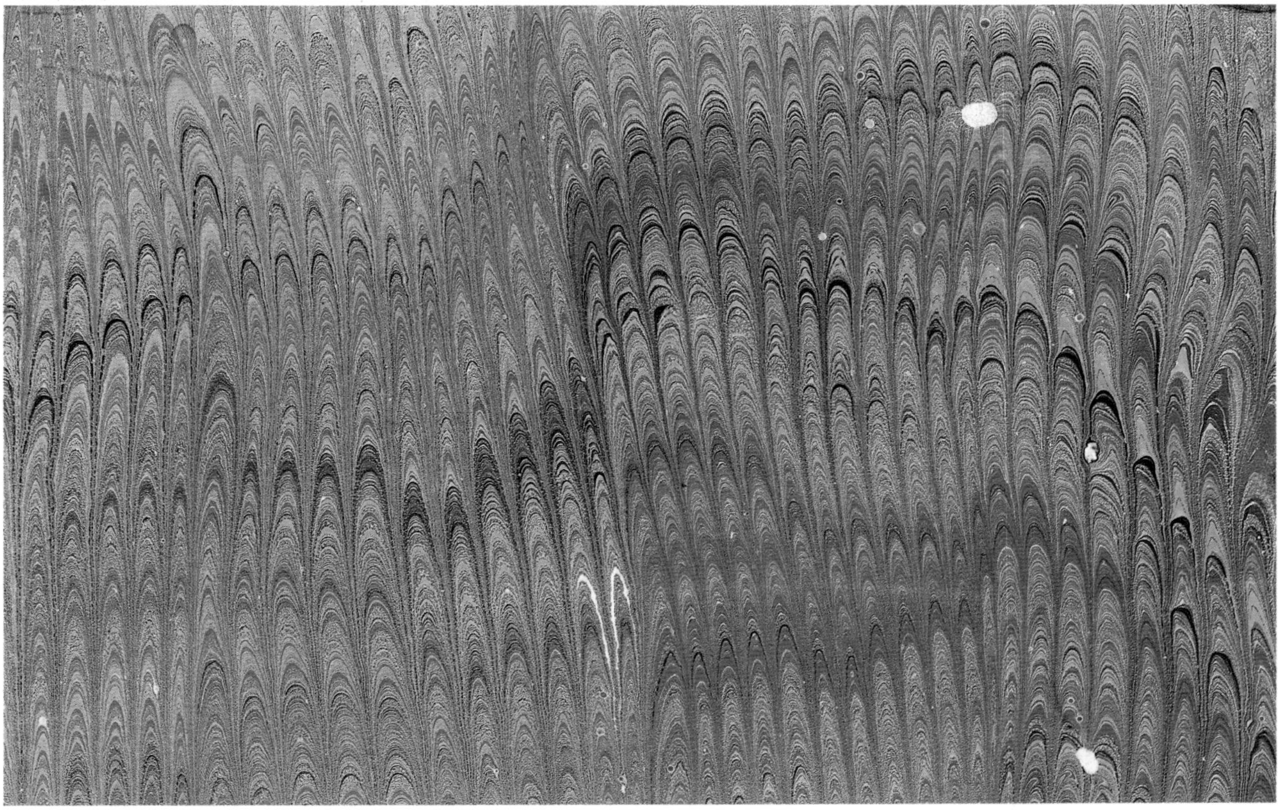

Using several colors of the same family will usually result in a poorly defined design.

you will get very sheer "Easter egg" colors. If you want a black and white sheet, this is easily made by applying black paint onto the surface of your size and then by lightly spattering on an extremely small amount of water to which has been added a few drops of your spreading medium or, if you are using an oil-based paint, by spattering on a very light sprinkling of turpentine or mineral spirits.

Metallic paints are created by adding bronzing powders to your paints—about one part bronzing powder to one part of your base paint. Your base paint should be a light color which will augment the gold powder, perhaps a yellow, a yellow ochre, or an orange. In order to get a truly stunning effect, you must use the metallic paint as your first color. That way, after you've added your second and third colors, your metallic base paint will become squeezed into the interstices and become brilliant and intense. If you would like to use your metallic as a top paint, you will find that it becomes very much dispersed, and although there may be somewhat a glistening effect, you will not get an immediate, reflective metallic look.

You would use an iridescent paint, or a paint to which you have added an iridescent powder, in a similar fashion. I also highly recommend a brand of French ready-to-use iridescent paints, imported by Savoir-Faire, called Texticolor Iridescent. These are wonderful paints for marbling; they only need thinning with water and are just as

effective when used on silk as when used on paper.

A wonderful look is obtained when you use a metallic or an iridescent paint on a dark-colored paper. This adds even more dimension to the effect because the metallics and the iridescents will be contrasted against the dark background. In fact, any type of marbling paint, when used on a colored paper background instead of the usual white, will give you pleasing, unexpected results. I recommend that you experiment using light marbled colors on a dark background. Certainly if you used a burgundy marbling paint on a brown paper, you would get scarcely visible results, so you need to opt for color combinations which will give you contrast.

When you are done marbling, you may want to consider covering your paints tightly so that they will keep for a later marbling session, instead of throwing them away. If you do discard them, though, it is wisest not to pour paint of any type down your drain.

In the following pages some basic directions are given for using four different types of paint. The sizes that are appropriate to them are included there also, but some materials can be used interchangeably and are not necessarily exclusive. For example, you can try using a carragheen size, normally used with watercolor and gouache, with tempera or acrylic paints instead. You can do some mixing and matching with interesting and exciting results.

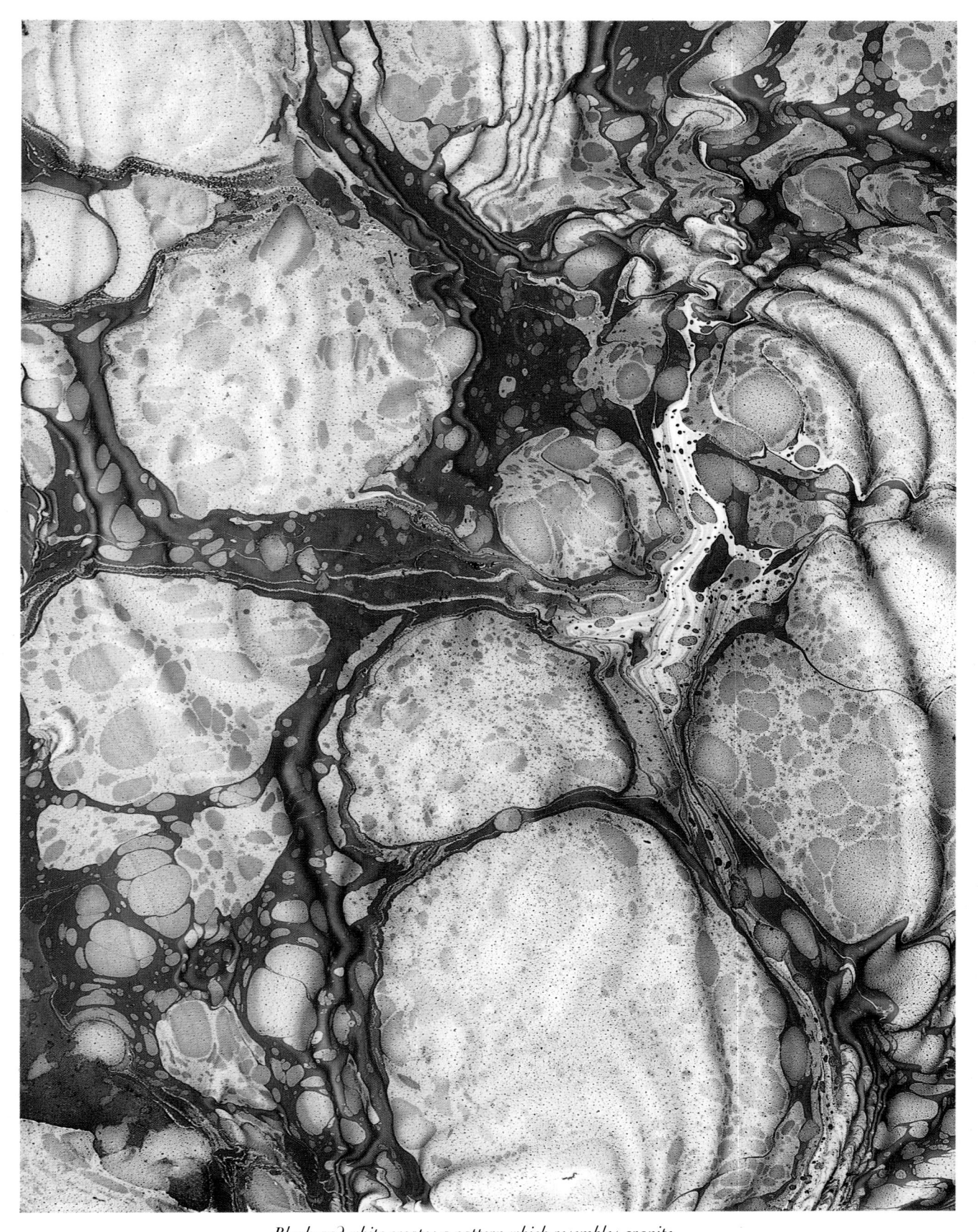

Black and white creates a pattern which resembles granite.

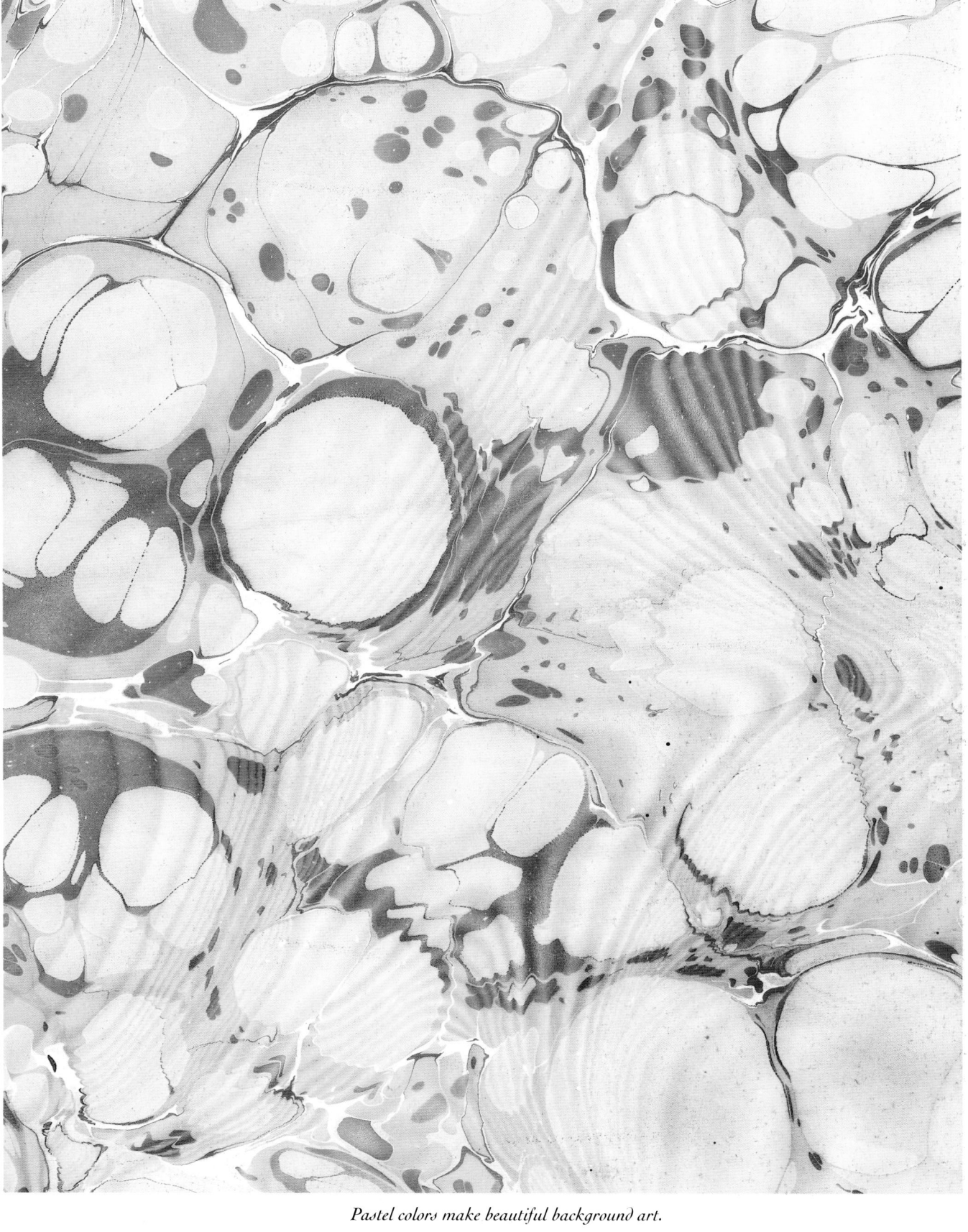

Pastel colors make beautiful background art.

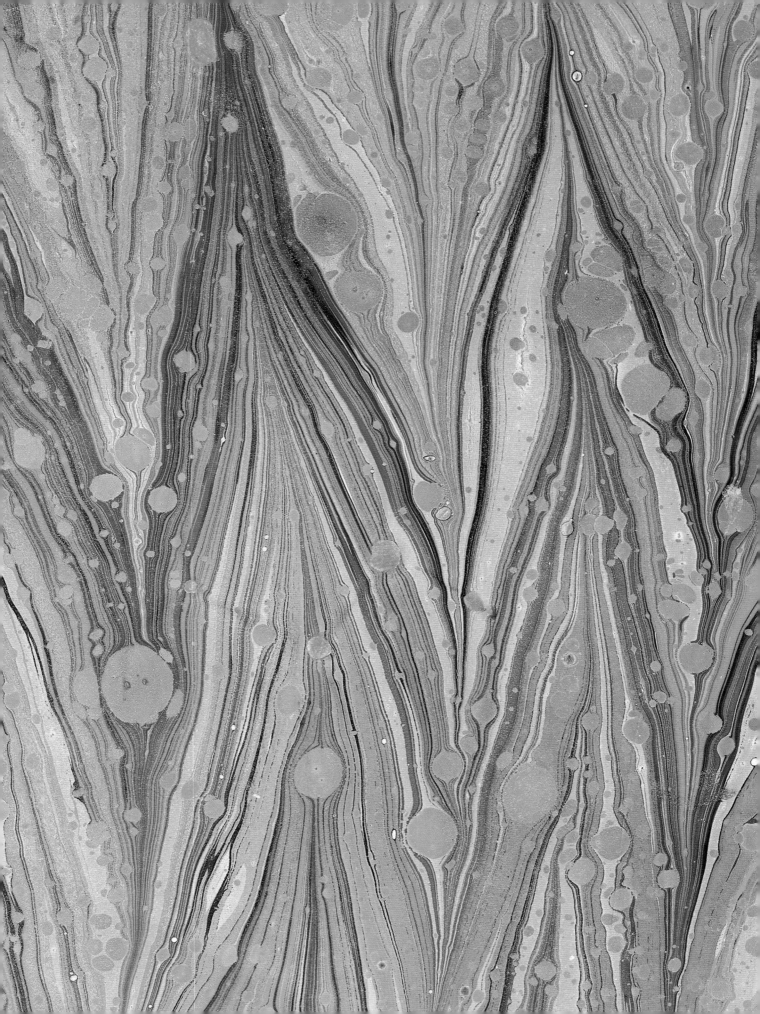

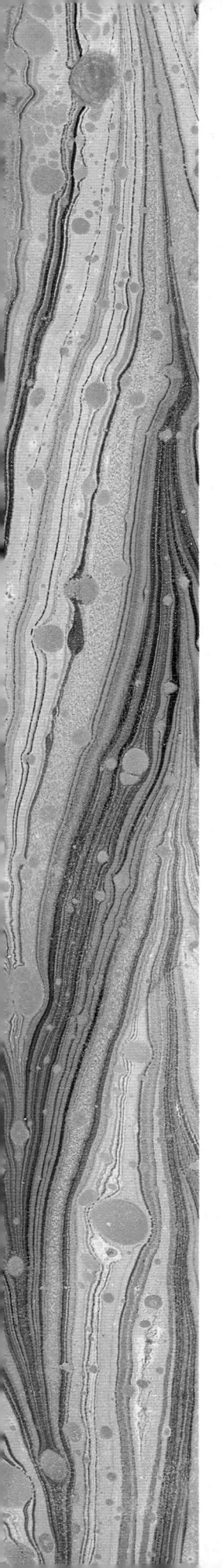

USING ACRYLICS

Marbling with acrylics will give you the same exquisite color and detail found in antique marbling, but without the headaches associated with using archaic materials. These new-age, polymer-based paints will produce superb traditional or experimental sheets. They are available in the consistency of watercolors and oils, and since they mix with water, it's easy to adjust their thickness for marbling. Another advantage is that acrylics are widely available, inexpensive, and easy to use.

Acrylic paints offer particularly brilliant hues.

As suggested under "Paper" on page 48, with acrylic paints you may need to prepare the paper with a mordant. Even so, I recommend that you see what results you get without it. Careful rinsing will be necessary.

After much research, I have found that the Portfolio line of marbling paints (manufactured by Savoir Faire) work more quickly and easily and are more foolproof than any other line of acrylics. Portfolio paints have been formulated for marbling particularly and are already tested and mixed with a spreading agent. You may use the Portfolio paints straight out of the bottle, with excellent results; they are ready-to-use.

If you prefer mixing your own paints from scratch, there is a brand of acrylic paint called Texticolor Opaque available in art- and craft-supply stores. (See the Sources section.) This product acts as a superb marbling paint. Thin this paint down until it is runny and add a drop or two of acrylic flow agent (a very good one is made by Winsor & Newton) to each cup. This acts to improve spreading, and can be used to increase the surface spread of any water-based paint, not just acrylic. This is an extremely powerful dispersant material, so use it *very sparingly.*

Both Portfolio and Texticolor work beautifully on papers of all kinds, and I recommend them for marbling on fabrics. Many other acrylics on the marketplace can be used, with varying results, by thinning with water and adding acrylic flow agent.

Portfolio's line of paints require no additives.

Texticolor acrylics come with a consistency closer to that of oils; they are opaque and require thinning.

Acrylic flow agent, added only a drop or two at a time, will facilitate the paint's spreading action.

Methocel is prepared like gelatin. It comes as a white powder.

Into a large, clean container that will hold 2 quarts or more, deposit about 4 rounded tablespoons of methocel.

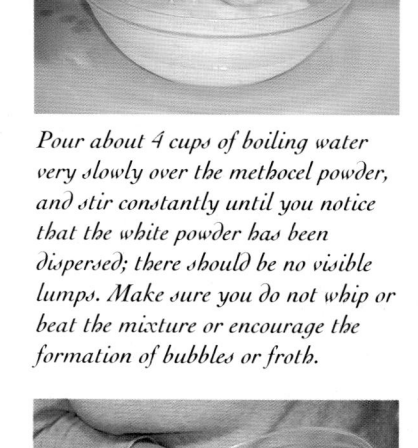

Pour about 4 cups of boiling water very slowly over the methocel powder, and stir constantly until you notice that the white powder has been dispersed; there should be no visible lumps. Make sure you do not whip or beat the mixture or encourage the formation of bubbles or froth.

You must then add 4 cups of ice water. The ice water may be made up completely or partially of ice cubes. Continue to stir gently until the mixture has been well blended.

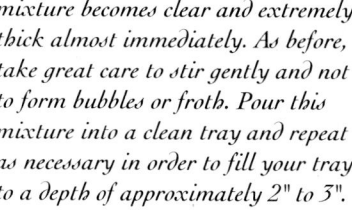

You will notice that the milky mixture becomes clear and extremely thick almost immediately. As before, take great care to stir gently and not to form bubbles or froth. Pour this mixture into a clean tray and repeat as necessary in order to fill your tray to a depth of approximately 2" to 3".

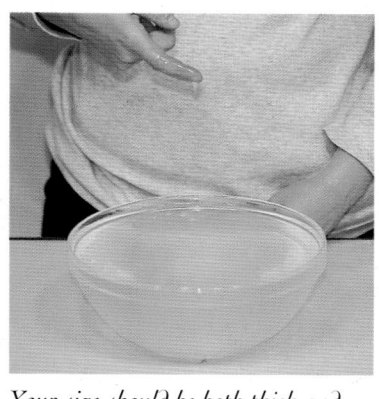

Your size should be both thick and pourable. If you test it with your finger, it should pick up a glistening coating of methocel which very slowly drips off. It will be approximately the thickness of pancake syrup. To thin it some, add cold water.

SIZE FOR ACRYLIC MARBLING

Portfolio also markets an excellent size base for marbling which is labeled "Instant Size Thickener." This is a 20th-century thickening agent commonly used in the food and drug industries. Its generic name is methocel.

Methocel has many amazing properties for the marbler to appreciate. First and foremost, it is easy to prepare—as simple as making gelatin. Methocel takes only ten minutes to prepare and is ready to use immediately. Unlike carragheen (described under "Using Watercolor and Gouache"), it does not need to rest for eight hours before it is workable—ideal for people who hate to wait. Methocel will also keep indefinitely in the tray without spoiling and getting watery. There is no need to refrigerate it; just keep it covered with plastic.

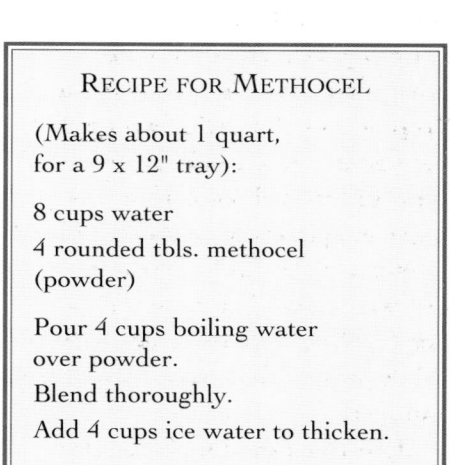

RECIPE FOR METHOCEL

(Makes about 1 quart, for a 9 x 12" tray):

8 cups water
4 rounded tbls. methocel (powder)

Pour 4 cups boiling water over powder.
Blend thoroughly.
Add 4 cups ice water to thicken.

USING WATERCOLOR AND GOUACHE

The most common materials used by marblers of the old school are traditional watercolors and gouaches. (Do not mistake new acrylic versions of these for the traditional ones.) The look achieved is clean-edged and precise; a great amount of detail is possible with excellent line quality. The drawbacks are that these materials are temperamental, and much time must be spent on adjusting paints, testing, and re-testing. Very subtle outside influences, such as the amount of oil on your skin, the amount of dust in the air, the temperature and humidity, and any residue left in your tray from other marbling sessions, may interfere greatly with the production of a successful sheet. This method is not for the faint of heart!

Gouache is simply an opaque form of the watercolor medium.

The paint I recommend you use, at least initially, is gouache, and it is available by the tube and jar. I recommend either Winsor & Newton or Talens, both of which offer a beautiful range of colors. There are two paint additives necessary (beyond the water used to thin the paints): alcohol and ox gall.

Squeeze about an inch-long deposit of paint into a clean glass container. With a small paintbrush or a broom corn whisk, thin this paint by adding approximately one teaspoon of water. Keep adding water until you have something that is about the consistency of cream. Add several drops of rubbing alcohol. You are now ready to add ox gall as a flow agent.

Ox gall is a by-product of the meat industry. It is literally the gall, or bile, secreted by the liver of a cow. It is a powerful dispersant material. There are several brands of ox gall sold in art-supply stores which will *not* work for marbling. Use only the *unfiltered* type, which has a brownish look and an extremely strong odor. The correct type of ox gall is available only by mail order. (See the Sources section for a list of companies you can buy it from.)

Add the ox gall drop by drop to your paints. If you add too much you will have a paint which spreads uncontrollably over the surface of the size. This will cause you just as many difficulties as having not enough spread. A little droplet of paint should start expanding the instant it hits the surface of the size, and it should expand to about 2" to 3" across, without leaving any sort of central leftover blob of paint.

Once you have mixed a set of four to five colors you like, you

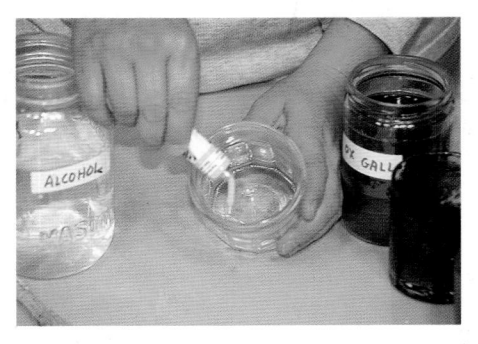

To a small deposit of gouache or watercolor . . .

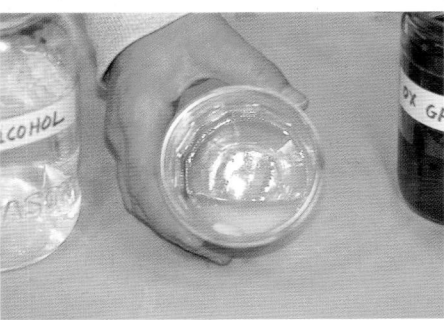

Add water and several drops of alcohol . . .

And a small quantity of dispersant ox gall to prepare gouache for marbling.

should create a few test sheets just to see how all your colors will work together. You may find that your final color (your last color applied), does not spread at all and that you need to begin again, testing and adjusting the ox gall. If your paints look particularly grainy, add a drop or two more of alcohol.

The very best paper for this type of marbling, as for acrylic marbling, is Lanaquarelle, imported from France. This cream-colored, 100-percent rag paper bears a striking resemblance to the type of papers used by some 19th-century marblers. In marbling with gouache, it is necessary to treat all of your paper with a mordant, as described under "Paper and Mordant," on page 46.

Fill your blender with water and add one level tablespoon of instant carragheen.

Hold the lid down tightly while blending, set at medium speed, for one to two full minutes.

Pour this bubbly mixture into a very clean tray. Repeat until you have made enough to fill your tray 2" to 3" deep.

Cover this tray of size with a clean sheet of plastic and let it rest for at least eight hours. When you return, the myriad tiny bubbles should have all risen to the surface. Before you begin to marble, you must take several sheets of newsprint the same size as your tray and lift this thick coating of bubbles off.

SIZE FOR WATERCOLOR AND GOUACHE

The size used with these water-based media is *carragheen* (also called Irish Moss), a seaweed grown off the coast of northern Europe. Once dried, it may be boiled and strained to produce a viscous liquid, but a more efficient method is to buy it in powder form and mix it up in a blender. One drawback is that it must be prepared eight hours beforehand and allowed to sit in a tray. It must also be used up within two to three days, before it spoils.

You must use up this tray of size within two to three days. You will know if your carragheen moss size has spoiled if it has become watery and has developed a somewhat fishy smell. The only thing that you can do with it at this point is to throw it away.

RECIPE FOR CARRAGHEEN

4 cups of water

1 level tbls. instant carragheen

Add carragheen to water.

Blend (preferably in blender set at medium) for 1-2 minutes.

Pour into tray.

Repeat as necessary.

Cover with plastic, let sit for 8 hours.

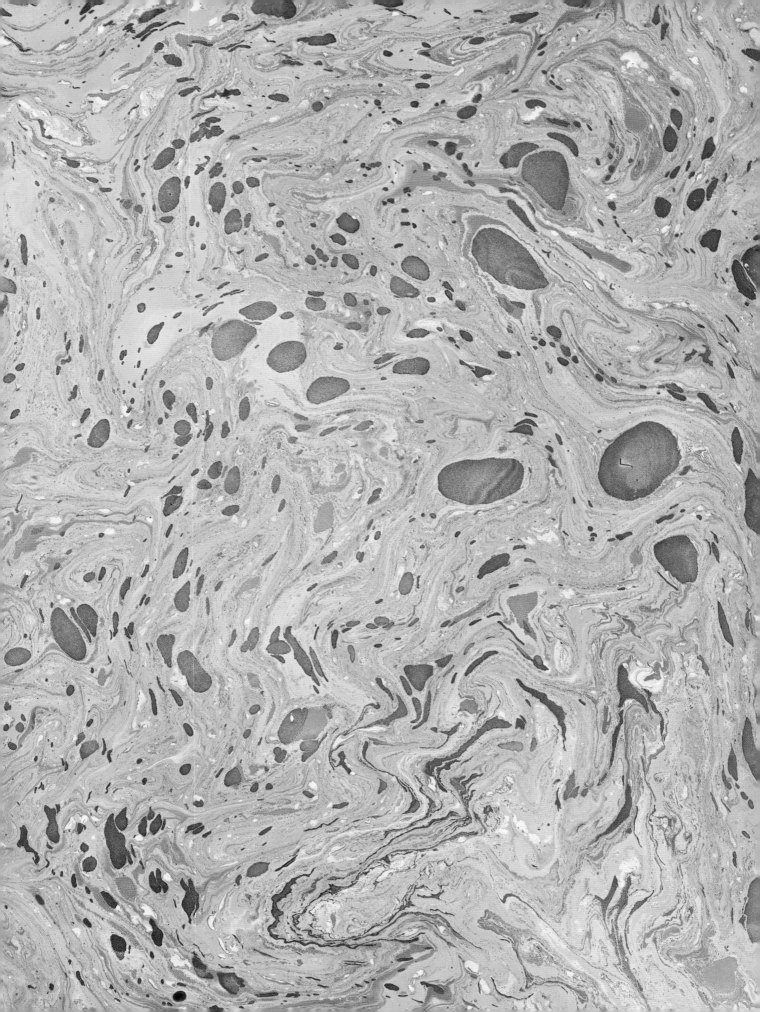

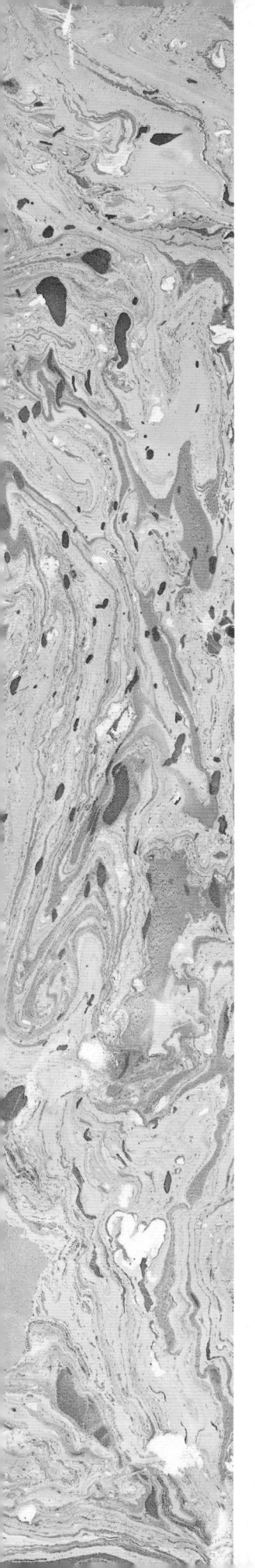

USING OIL PAINTS

Oil paints can be messy and smelly sometimes. The paints themselves must be mixed or thinned with turpentine or mineral spirits, solvents to which many people have adverse reactions. However, there are some wonderful benefits to using oil-based paints, in spite of their smell. Oils create gorgeous free-form marbled designs that you cannot get with any other type of paint. They are great for experimental work and will create textures and forms all by themselves that will dazzle you. You will never get the hard-edged line quality that you get with acrylics or gouache paints; with oils you have to enjoy the accident-of-the-moment approach and appreciate the serendipity of the outcome.

Oil-based paints yield an organic look.

Another nice thing about oil-based marbling is that it is not a "temperamental" method. Once they are mixed to the right consistency, oil paints will reliably float on the surface of your water-based size, because oil and water will not mix.

Just about any brand of oil paint that you can find on the market works well in marbling. I've gotten especially good results with Winsor & Newton and Sennelier, two brands that seem to have a very finely ground pigment that thins well with turpentine.

You can use oil paints on any size that is mentioned in this book. After you've created your size and skimmed off the bubbles, you can start to mix up your paints. Squeeze about an inch-long deposit of paint into a clean glass jar, add very small amounts of turpentine or paint thinner (mineral spirits), and mix this

very well with a brush or a broom corn whisk, until they are "drippy." If you use a brush, find one with an extremely long flange of somewhat droopy hairs; this will tend to pick up large droplets of paint and sprinkle them on in a mixture of large and small drops (sometimes these are called "drop" brushes). You will notice when you drop oil paints onto the surface of your size that the thicker your paints are, the heavier they become and the more likely they are to drop through the surface. You may then need to give yourself a fairly thick size in order to support the oil paints. If you find you have continual problems with your oil paints dropping through the surface, you may want to try thinning the paints down just a little bit more.

In your choice of papers, you have complete latitude with oil paints, for they will settle in and

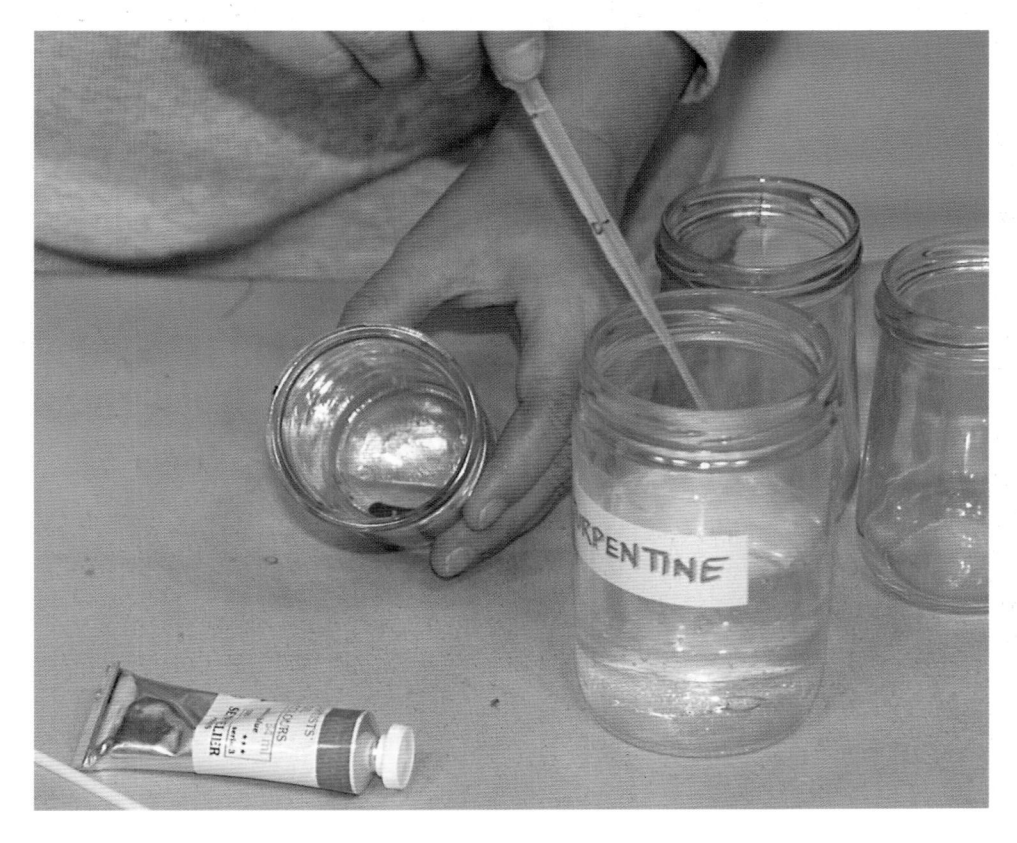

Turpentine is the usual thinner and dispersant for oil paints, but you can also use paint thinner (mineral spirits), a petroleum distillate with a weaker odor.

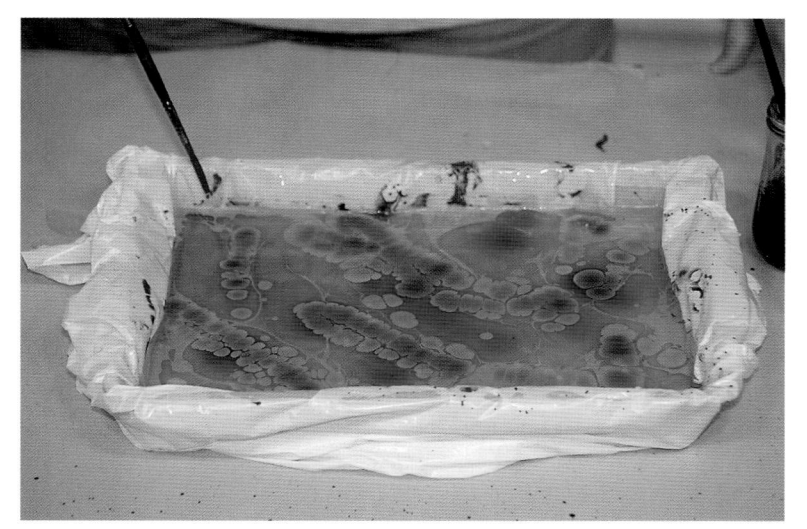

Oil paints can create strange, organic shapes...

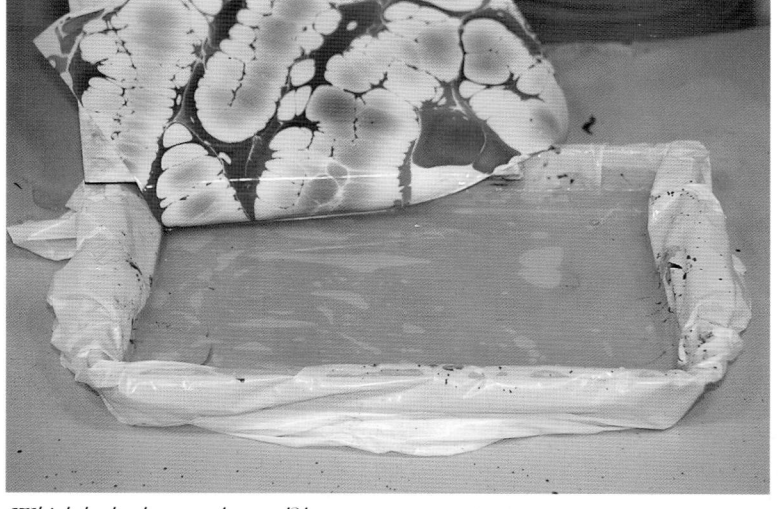

Which look almost otherworldly...

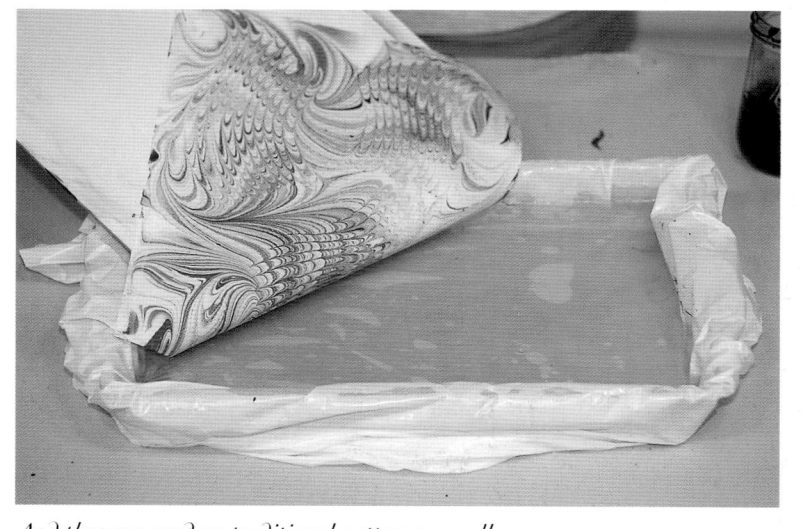

And they can produce traditional patterns as well.

attach themselves to virtually any paper out there. There is never any need to treat your paper with alum or prepare it in any way. The only kind of paper you cannot use is, as usual, a plastic-coated paper.

One thing that you absolutely have to remember when you marble with oils is to have adequate ventilation. After years of experimenting in my own studio I finally rigged up a very effective ventilation system: I placed my marbling table in front of a window with an attic fan, which sucked the fumes right out before they even rose to the level of my face.

You also have to remember that when you are working with oil paints or solvents, you are dealing with very flammable material. Take great care in depositing all your cleanup rags in a safe way, preferably outside the building.

As mentioned earlier, oil paints are more unpredictable than water-based paints, including acrylics. This makes them especially attractive to people who love to experiment. You can use tube oil paints, block printing inks, or offset printing inks. Add bronzing powders to your oil paints for all kinds of wonderful metallic looks, or try adding different types of oil painting mediums into your paint mixture. You will get entirely new and wonderful effects each time.

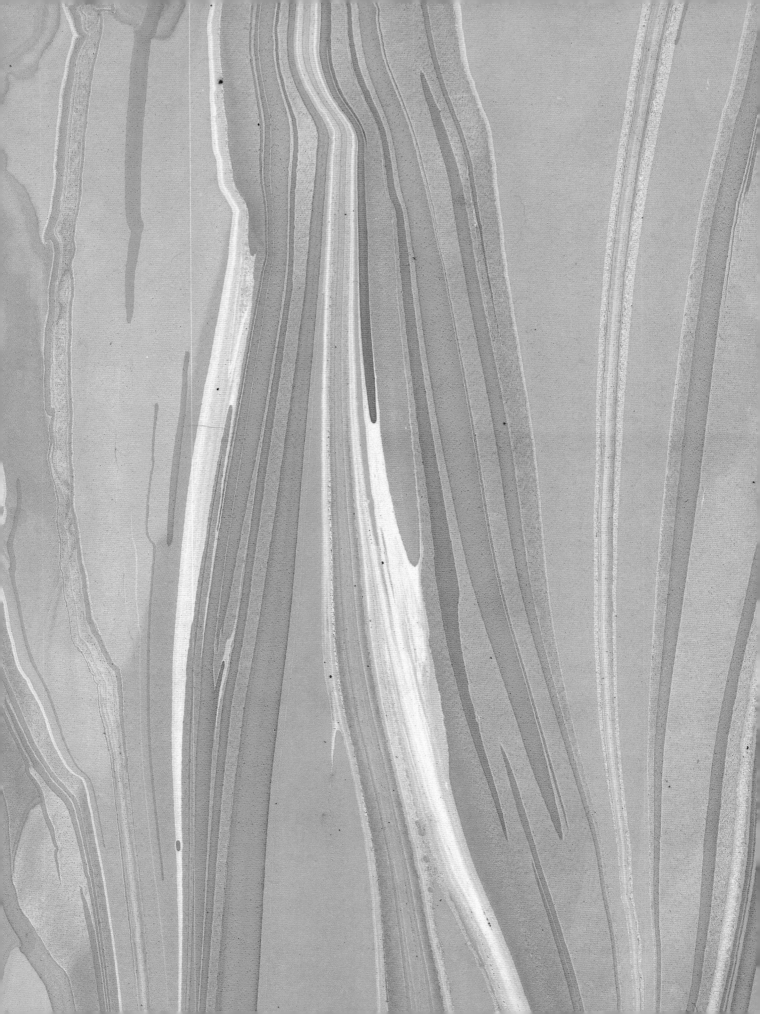

USING TEMPERA

The fine-art term "tempera" properly applies to a paint made by combining pigments with an emulsion, which is basically a mixture of water and an oily, fatty, waxy, or resinous substance. The traditional tempera emulsion is egg yolk, and an oil like linseed oil has long been included in the mixture. Gum arabic and beeswax have been used instead of egg yolk. But "tempera" is also loosely applied to a range of ready-made paints sold in tubes, bottles, and even in a powder, as shown below, that you mix with water. Popularly known as poster paints, their quality varies widely, so you should experiment with different products to find one that gives you consistently good results.

Tempera's slightly grainy texture can produce dramatic results.

This marbling medium is perhaps the very simplest of all. Water-based tempera paints are particularly wonderful for marbling with children or beginners. The materials are very easy to get and are entirely nontoxic. Their main limitation is that they are somewhat grainy, so one must be satisfied with rather large design motifs.

Thin your tempera paints with water, using clean glass jars, paper cups (these are fine for tempera), or muffin tins for mixing. They should be about the consistency of cream. Add a few drops of a spreading agent, such as Winsor & Newton's acrylic flow improver, to each color. You may also try a very handy substitute—soap. Soap will have the same dispersant effect, but use a tiny amount, or else you may end up with bubbly paints.

You can use any kind of paper you want to with tempera, and if you're teaching children, don't hesitate to use newsprint or manila paper. Manila paper marbles beautifully and gives a creamy background color to all your designs.

CORNSTARCH SIZE FOR TEMPERA MARBLING

Use a cornstarch-based size with tempera paints. You can create your own thickened base by cooking the powdered cornstarch, or you can buy cornstarch already mixed and ready to use. (It goes under the label Vano Starch.)

Cornstarch size will spoil after about four to six days.

Here, tempera paints hit the surface of the cornstarch size.

A spreading medium such as soap will keep them from clumping.

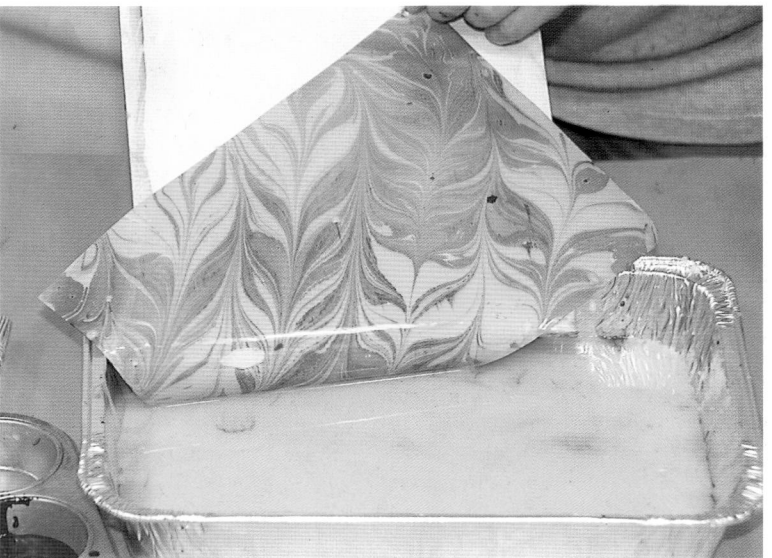

Making a broad combed pattern in tempera paints.

Here is a diagonal Back and Forth pattern enlivened by complementary colors.

To mix the size yourself, use 1 cup of a powdered cornstarch such as Kingsford, mix it up well with about 1 cup of cold water and pour it in your tray. Bring 3 to 4 quarts of water to an extremely rapid boil. Pour your cornstarch mixture into your tray (your tray must be hard plastic or metal). Quickly pour 2 to 3 quarts of your boiling water into your tray and immediately begin stirring with a slotted spoon. You must continue to do so for about 5 minutes to prevent the formation of clumps of cornstarch. Add boiling water until you have approximately the consistency of buttermilk or gravy. You must let this tray of cornstarch sit until it is cool; it may thicken somewhat as it cools. If you do have a problem with lumps, you can go back through your cornstarch and lift them out with the slotted spoon.

RECIPE FOR CORNSTARCH SIZE

3 to 4 quarts water
1 cup cornstarch

Mix the cornstarch first with
    1 cup of cold water.
Add 2 quarts of boiling water.
Stir well.
Add water if necessary to thin.

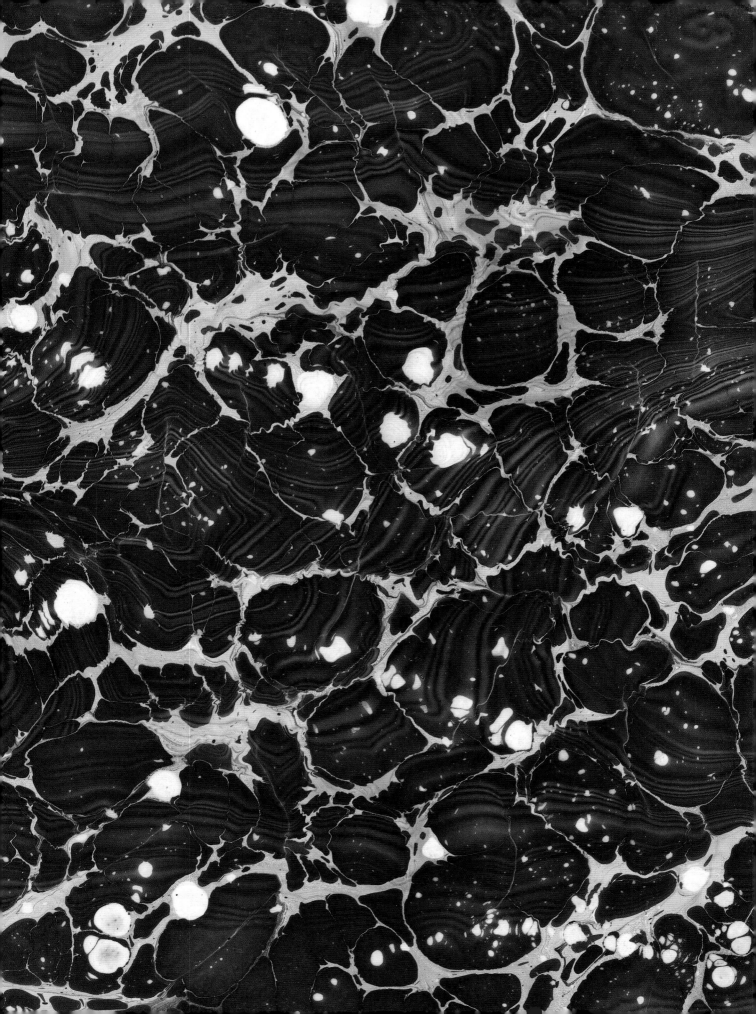

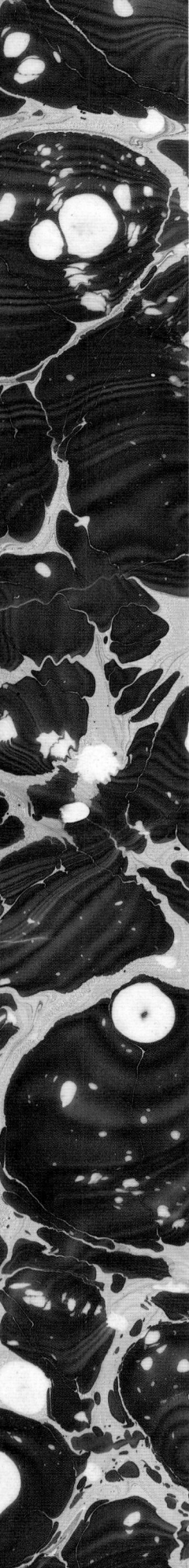

THE WORKSPACE

When marbling, you must plan your workspace for cleanliness, safety, and efficiency. Most of the materials for marbling are fairly safe and nontoxic. However, all marbling size is extremely slippery and can present a definite hazard when dripped on the floor. Be extremely careful, and cover your floor with newspapers or carpet scraps. Carpet scraps will always work best; they have a tendency to soak up some of the dripped size and prevent you from slipping. Very close at hand, you will need a large trash can for paper you are using in cleaning up, your reject sheets, and so forth. You do not want a trash can far away, forcing you to carry dripping papers that leave a messy trail.

NEWSPAPERS   MARBLING TRAY AND PAINTS   MARBLING PAPERS

∧ *An orderly arrangement of tools and materials will pay off in efficiency.*

< *Marbled by the author, this sheet gets its unique quality from the veining.*

75

Create a triangle layout in your workspace, with your marbling table at the first station; here you have your tray, paper, and paints. Your second station should be a rinsing station, where you will be rinsing and scraping your papers off. Your third station should be your drying station, where you are going to hang your papers up.

Placed close at hand, along with your marbling papers, have a stack of newspapers cut to the inside dimensions of your marbling tray.

One further note regarding safety: If you are using oil paints, don't forget how important ventilation is. Set up a window fan to suck the fumes out of your work area.

RINSING AND DRYING STATION

Your rinsing station could be organized in several different ways. Professional marblers have a deep sink (frequently a laundry sink) with a large board set up at a diagonal in it. The freshly marbled paper is quickly laid onto the slanted rinsing board, and a spray nozzle is used to rinse the leftover size off the marbled sheet.

You should remember, whether you are using a spray nozzle or water coming directly out of a faucet or hose, that if you direct a jet or spray of water directly onto a sheet of freshly marbled paper, the force of the water may wipe out an area of your design and create a whitened spot. Also, your paper should be held not fully vertical but at a bit of an angle.

There are other ways of creating an effective rinsing station if you do not have plumbing for a sink. Probably the easiest would be to have a large plastic tub filled with clean

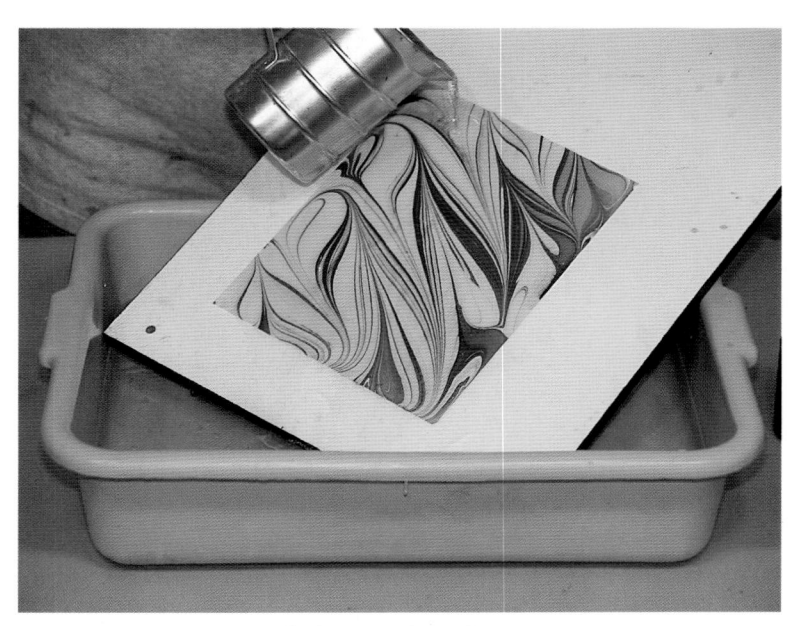

Don't consider the paint to be fixed until it is dry.

Keep your rinsing board in an almost vertical position.

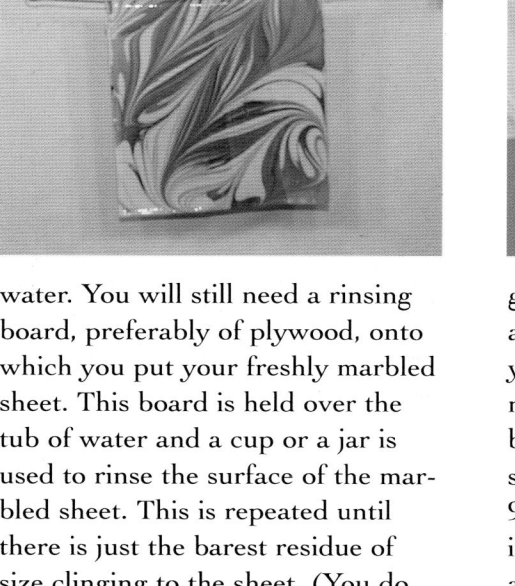

water. You will still need a rinsing
board, preferably of plywood, onto
which you put your freshly marbled
sheet. This board is held over the
tub of water and a cup or a jar is
used to rinse the surface of the marbled sheet. This is repeated until
there is just the barest residue of
size clinging to the sheet. (You do
not have to remove every vestige of
size from your marbled paper.)
After you have rinsed the paper,
you will need to hang it up to dry.

Drying racks can be easily set up
using string or twine which has
been stretched across any sort of
framework. The only drawback to
this method is that it will not hold a

great quantity of paper, so if you
are doing a lot of production work
you will want to set up something
more commodious. If you are marbling with children or marbling on
small pieces of paper (8½ x 11",
9 x 12" or so), a handy way of drying is to drape each wet sheet over
a wire hanger. Another handy
method is to use an old-fashioned
wood laundry-drying rack. This
folding rack is available at hardware and housewares stores.

Included in the illustrations here
is a design for a professional drying
rack which is very easily and cheap-
ly made out of plastic piping and
wooden dowels. Create the framework in any dimension you like,
simply attaching the pieces together
as if you were using Tinkertoys,
and drape each freshly marbled
sheet over one of the dowels.
Another benefit to the plastic piping
is that you can disassemble it after
you are done marbling and put it
away. When setting up your drying
rack you should put some sort of
absorbent material underneath it—
either a piece of carpet scrap or several layers of newspapers, which
you can roll up and throw away
afterward.

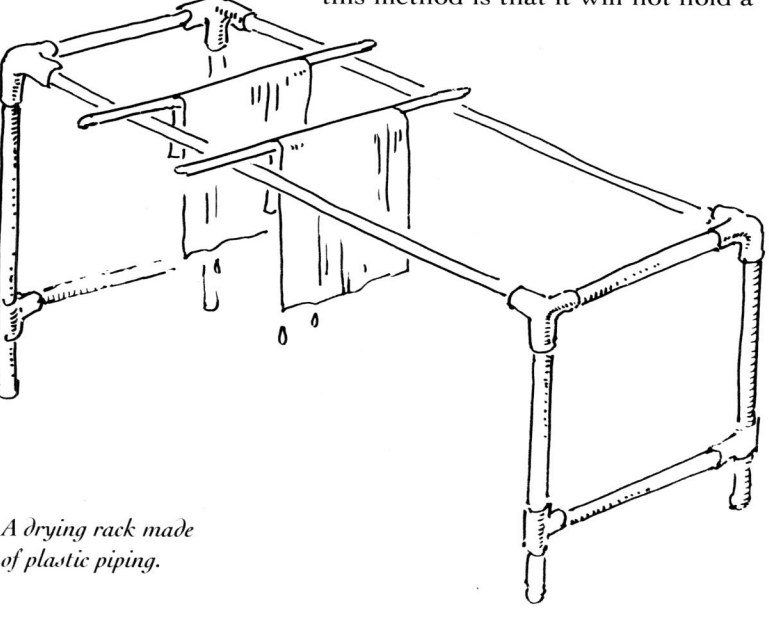

*A drying rack made
of plastic piping.*

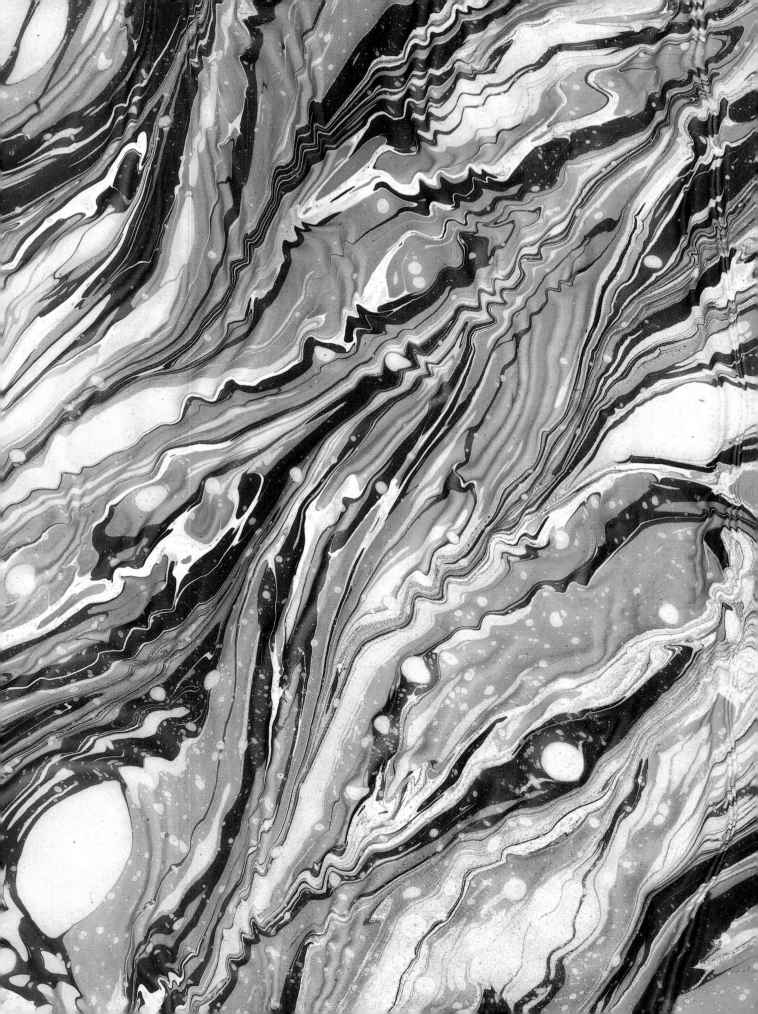

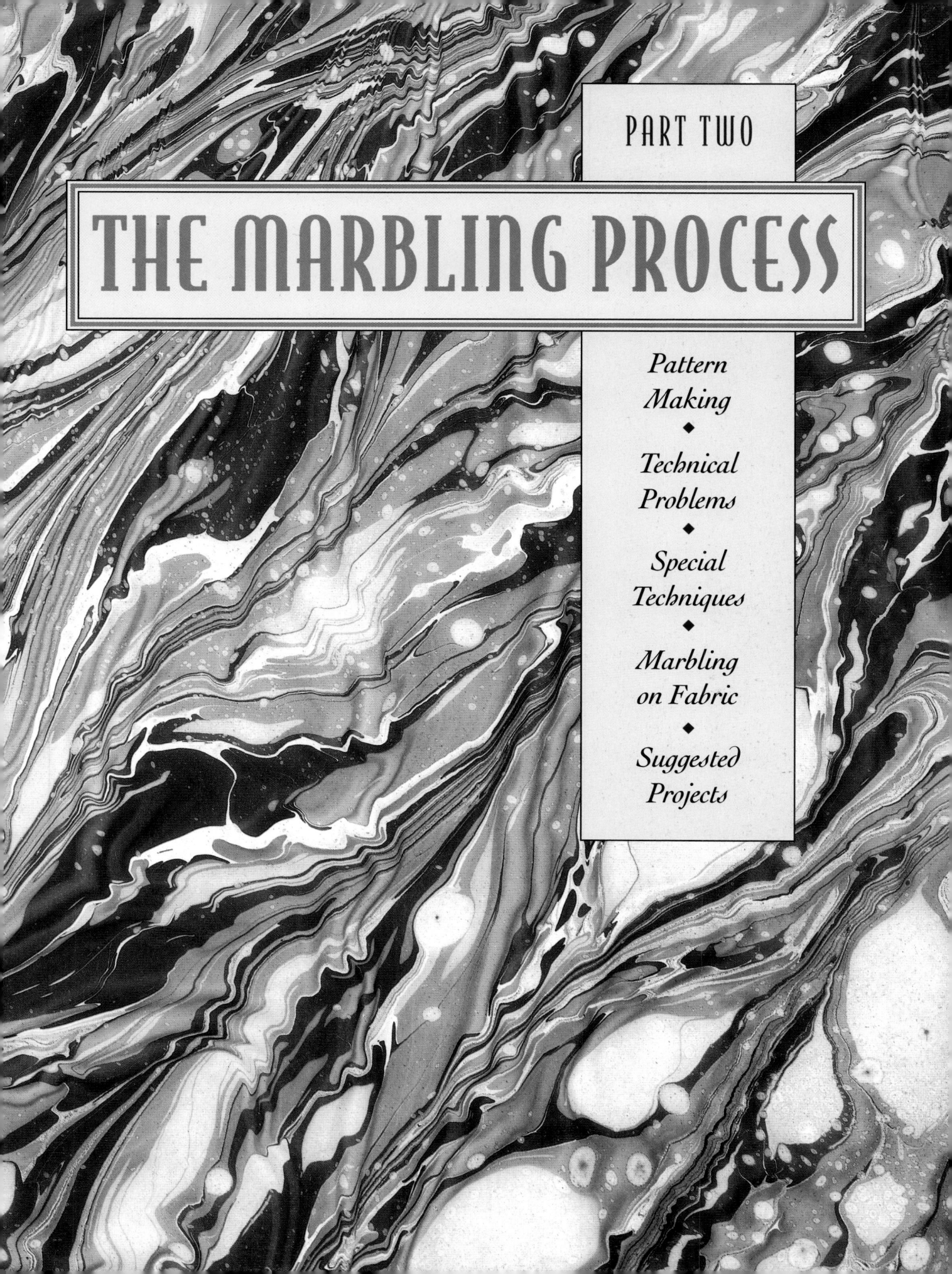

PART TWO

THE MARBLING PROCESS

Pattern
Making

◆

Technical
Problems

◆

Special
Techniques

◆

Marbling
on Fabric

◆

Suggested
Projects

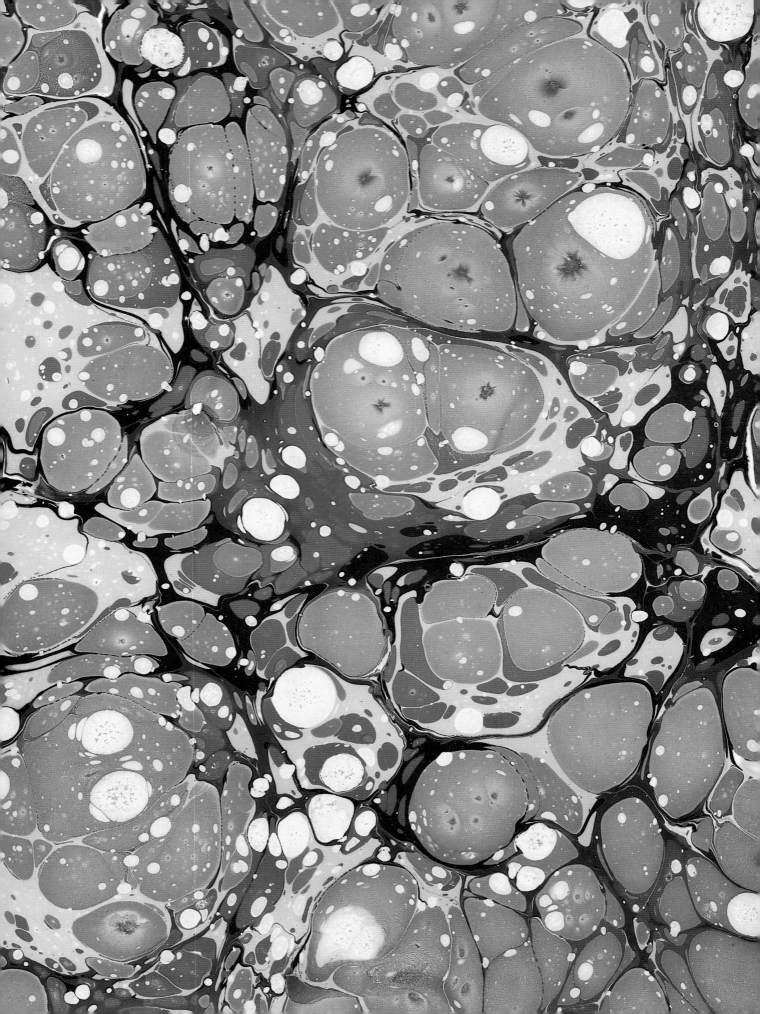

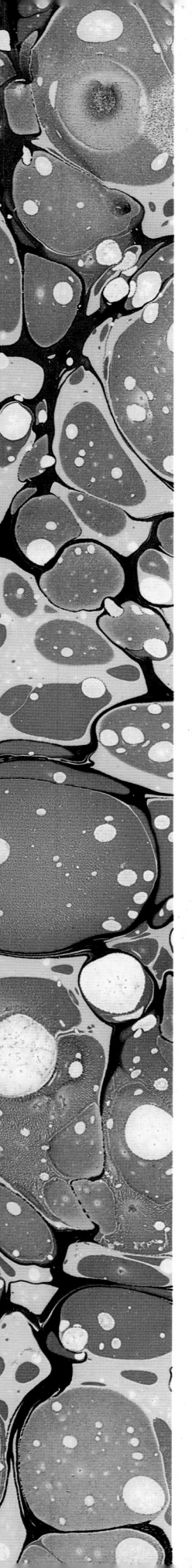

PATTERN MAKING

Crucial to the marbling process is getting your paints to do two things: float, and then spread, on the surface of the size. If you cannot control these two things, you cannot create any sort of pattern other than random and accidental ones. It helps beginners to understand that, when marbling, you are in effect painting on a ground. However, the ground is neither paper nor canvas, but the plane of the size's surface. The surface tension of this plane is very delicate, and if you overload it, your paint will break through and simply sink to the bottom of the tray. As you learn about the creation of beautiful patterns, heed the guidelines concerning the tricky alliance that must be maintained between the size and the paints.

∧ *A French Snail pattern, ready for rinsing.*

< *The Turkish Stone is the simplest pattern of all and perhaps the most beautiful.*

Turkish Stone

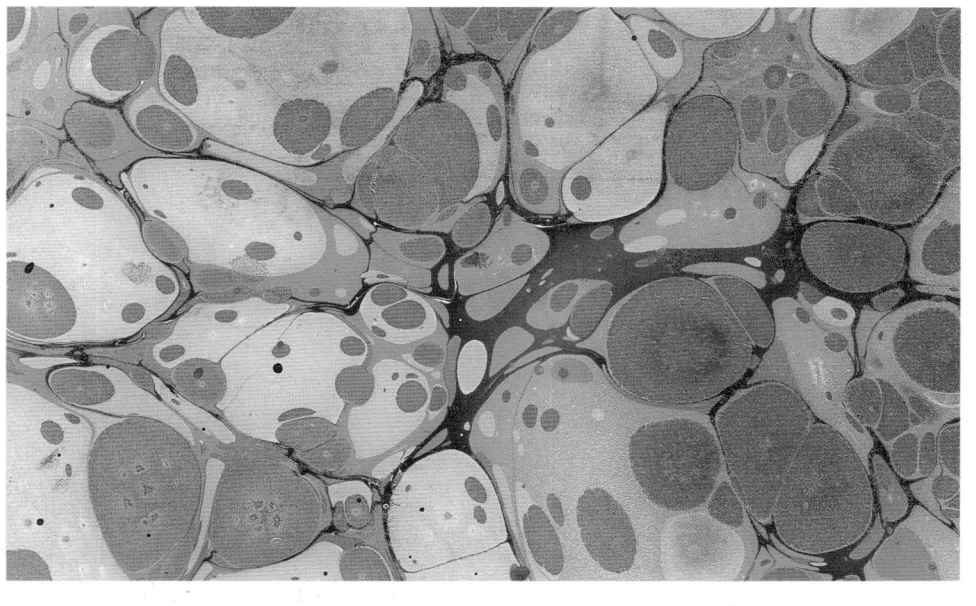

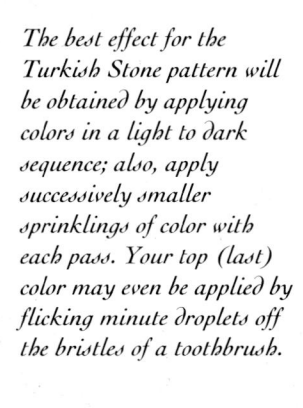

The best effect for the Turkish Stone pattern will be obtained by applying colors in a light to dark sequence; also, apply successively smaller sprinklings of color with each pass. Your top (last) color may even be applied by flicking minute droplets off the bristles of a toothbrush.

All the elaborate combed patterns you have seen inside the covers of old books begin with the most ancient pattern of all—the Turkish Stone. That is, the creation of all combed patterns is done by raking a comb or stylus through a floating Turkish Stone pattern. Learning patterning must always begin there.

Some of the more complicated patterns require three or four passes over the paint, and one must *work quickly* to finish up the design before the paints begin to break down and you lose your line quality. Beginning marblers should try to remember to quit when they are ahead. This applies to the addition of too many colors as well.

The simplest and boldest patterns are usually the most stunning and many a good design has been ruined by "just one more pass" with the stylus. After a certain amount of manipulation, marbling paints begin to mix together into a muddy mess—the marbler's nightmare.

You should have tested your size and paints as instructed, and now you are ready to mix up four or five colors to work with. Make sure that you have a varied palette—warm and cool colors, dark and light colors. In order to end up with a good pattern, you must have colors which will contrast with each other.

Throughout the process, when using either a comb or a stylus, you should take great care to keep your hand steadily and evenly moving along. Avoid jerky, quick, or stirring motions.

As you read the steps to take in creating the classic seven patterns below, examine the illustrations for an understanding of the end result toward which you are working. For now, we will make marbled papers, but you can pick up patterned paint on silk also; this is explained under "Marbling on Fabric," page 117.

Step 1. When applying paints, less is more!

Step 2. Marbling is a forgiving craft: if you make a mistake, you can pick it up by inserting a paper tab. The design is self-healing and will close up.

Step 3. Work evenly and quickly. Between applications of colors, let them spread for a few seconds.

Step 1. The broom corn whisk is the ideal tool for creating the variegated spots necessary to a good Turkish Stone. Using your whisk, pick up a small amount of paint on the bristles' ends and spatter it *gently* onto the surface of your size by knocking or tapping the whisk against your finger. Your hands should be 6" to 8" above the tray and moving quickly as you go.

Step 2. The droplets will begin to expand immediately, until they are almost contiguous. If your paints are not spreading effectively, thin your size slightly or add a few drops of your spreading agent to your paints. This first layer of paint should be very sheer, but don't be fooled—this first color will become the most brilliant in the final sheet. This is the result of successive layers of paint squeezing the first into the interstices, creating a veining effect. Since this veining is so essential, try using a deep or dark color as your first one, such as black, blue, or deep red.

Step 3. As soon as your first color has stopped spreading (this should take only eight to ten seconds), use a clean broom corn whisk to apply, in the same manner, your second and then third colors. Again, try to use your colors in a light–dark or warm–cool sequence (or a combination of the two), and remember to distribute your colors evenly across the surface of your size, not just in the center.

Apply your paints *sparingly* and keep a very close eye on the droplets. When you see that the spreading action has slowed down considerably, *stop!* It is a sign that the surface has been fully loaded, and the addition of any more paint may cause sinking and mixing.

Step 4. After three or four applications of paint, you should have a one-of-a-kind design floating like a veil on the watery surface.

Step 5. Pick up your paper on opposite sides and, keeping it in a slight curve, gently but quickly lay it down upon the surface.

Step 6. Do not press it down; instead, lower it until the middle of the sheet makes contact with the paint. Then instantly let go of the paper, making sure not to trap any air under the surface.

Step 4. Limit your palette to no more than three or four colors.

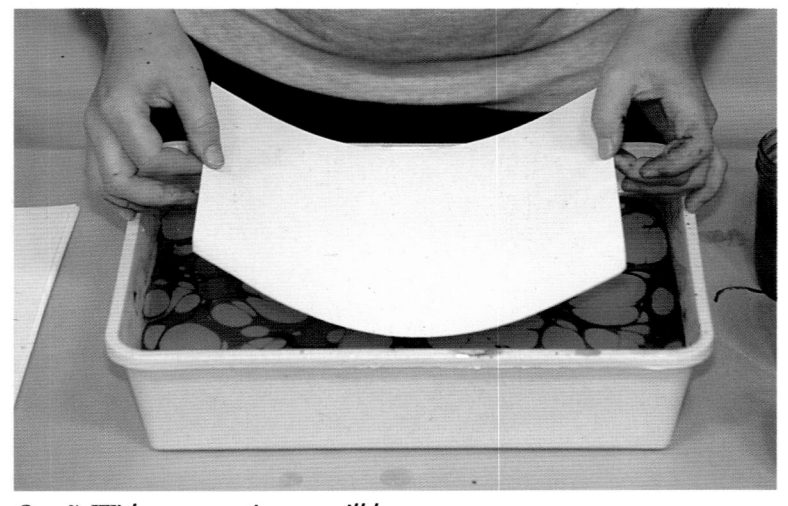

Step 5. With some practice, you will lay your paper down with one smooth motion.

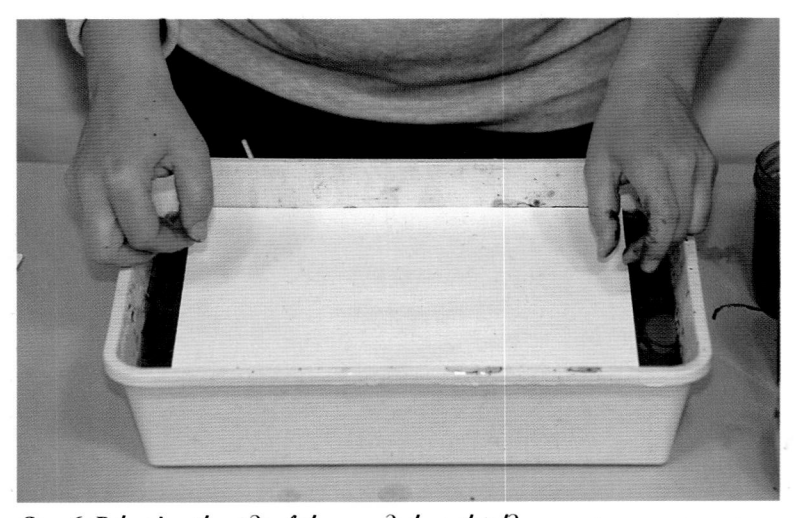

Step 6. Releasing the ends of the curved sheet should prevent the trapping of air beneath it.

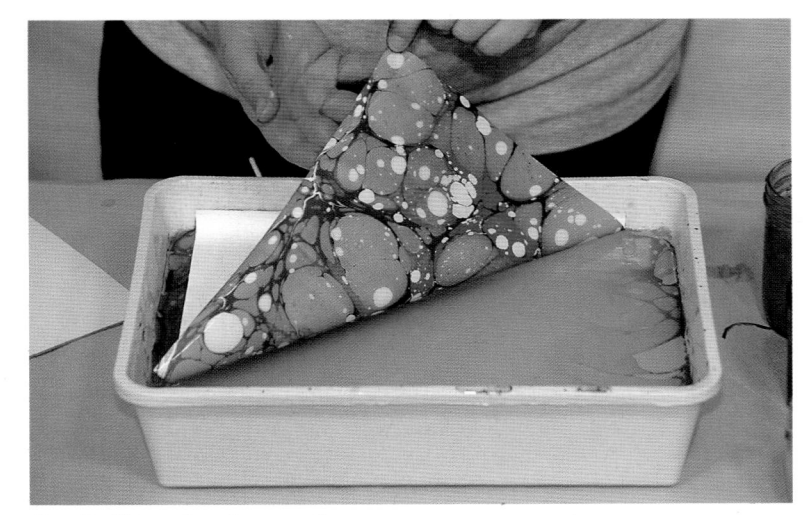

Step 7. After only a few seconds, you may see your creation.

Step 8. Immediately place the sheet on a sturdy rinsing board.

Step 9. A piece of ragboard, the edge softened with water, can be used to gently scrape off excess size. If you begin to see scrape marks, try rinsing instead.

Step 7. There is no need to leave the paper on for more than a few seconds. Lift the sheet up again—the magic is done!

Step 8. After you pick the sheet up, lay it flat on a rinsing board (see page 74), paint side up, and rinse it under a gentle stream of water. Do not direct a stream straight onto it, for this may mar the paint. Keep the board angled, but nearly vertical, as the water flows over it. You should *never rub* in an effort to remove the remaining size clinging to the surface. The paint is not fixed until it is dry. Some leftover size will do no harm. You may now hang your sheet up to dry, which will take about two hours.

Step 9. If you do not have an adequate rinsing situation, here is a shortcut you may use. I have found, in doing many sales floor demonstrations, that you may use a piece of cardboard, preferably ragboard, approximately 2 x 8". Wet one of the long edges and gently scrape off the excess size of a sheet that is laid flat on a smooth board. Use a very light hand, and take care not to scrape off the paint also. This is an easy method, especially if you are using small marbled sheets, and it works well with children.

All the following patterns must begin by applying paints for stone marbling (that is, for creating a Turkish Stone).

Back and Forth

Also known by its Turkish name, Get-gel, this pattern is created by first spattering on colors as for stone marbling. After doing this, insert your stylus 1/4" through the surface paint in one corner and slowly drag it back and forth—first vertically, all the way up and down the tray, and then horizontally. This process is demonstrated in the illustrations shown here.

Always start with a Turkish Stone pattern.

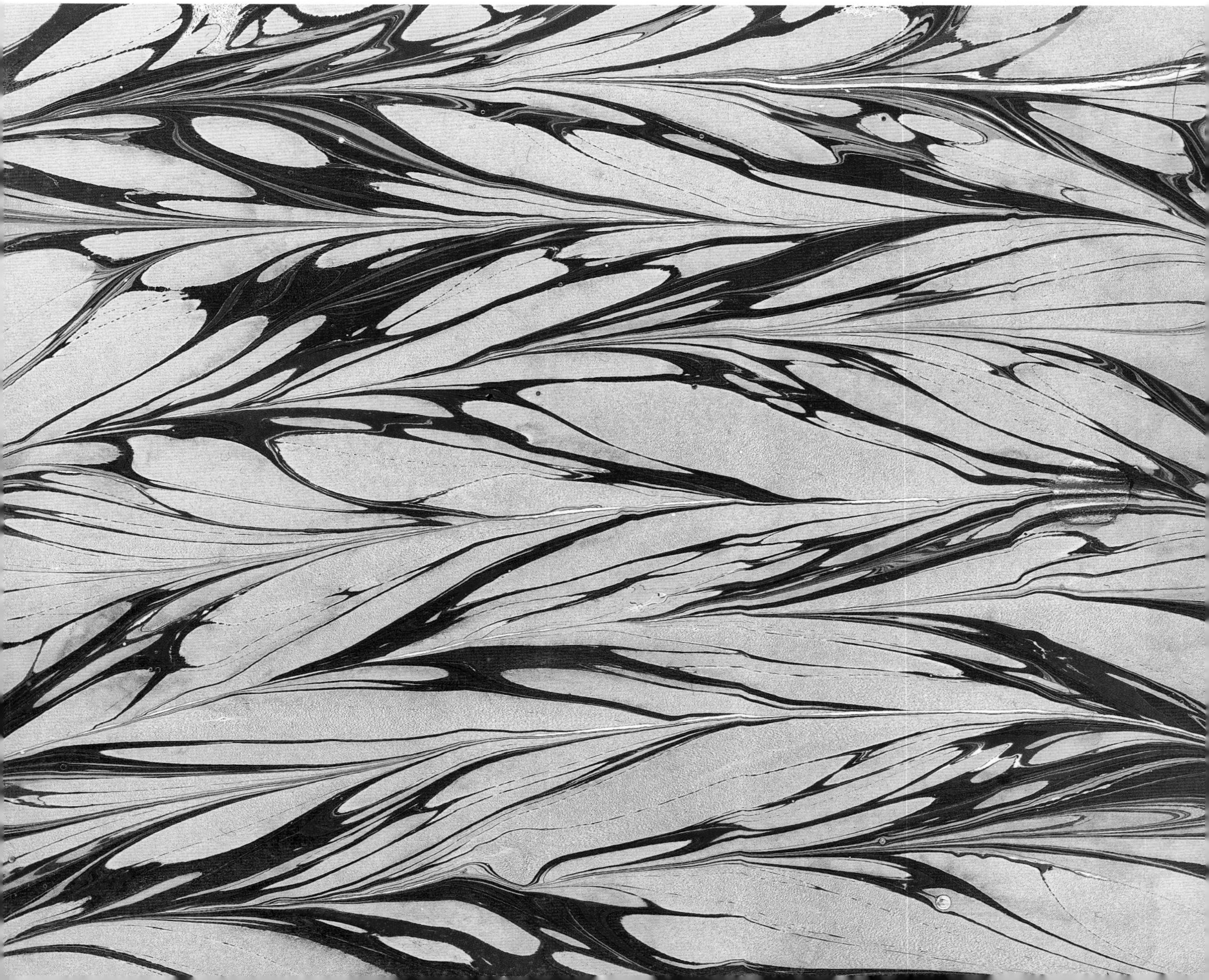

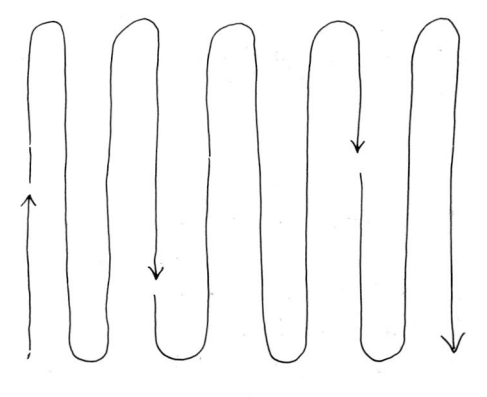

Do not let the stylus touch the bottom of the tray but only penetrate the top layer by about 1/4".

Move quickly but smoothly.

The chevron effect is stunning.

Antique Spot, or Zebra

Start with a Back and Forth pattern, but as you are moving your stylus about, give a slight wiggle to the line. When you are done with the back-and-forth motions, take a very small amount of a top color (a lighter color preferably) on the ends of your broom corn and spatter a very fine sprinkling of paints on top of your Back and Forth pattern. A toothbrush also works well to apply the very tiniest of sprinklings.

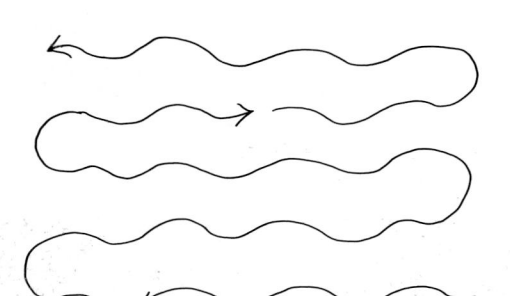

The Antique Spot, or Zebra, pattern is a close relative of the Back and Forth.

The Curtain

Create the Back and Forth pattern as described and, using your stylus, pull against the grain of your design. Pull toward you across the tray repeatedly at about 1" to 2" intervals. This will create a beautiful three-dimensional drapery look.

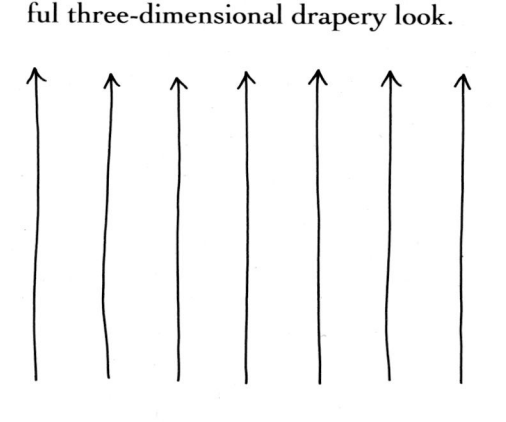

Once again, pull against the pattern of a Back and Forth. The Curtain pattern has a three-dimensional effect.

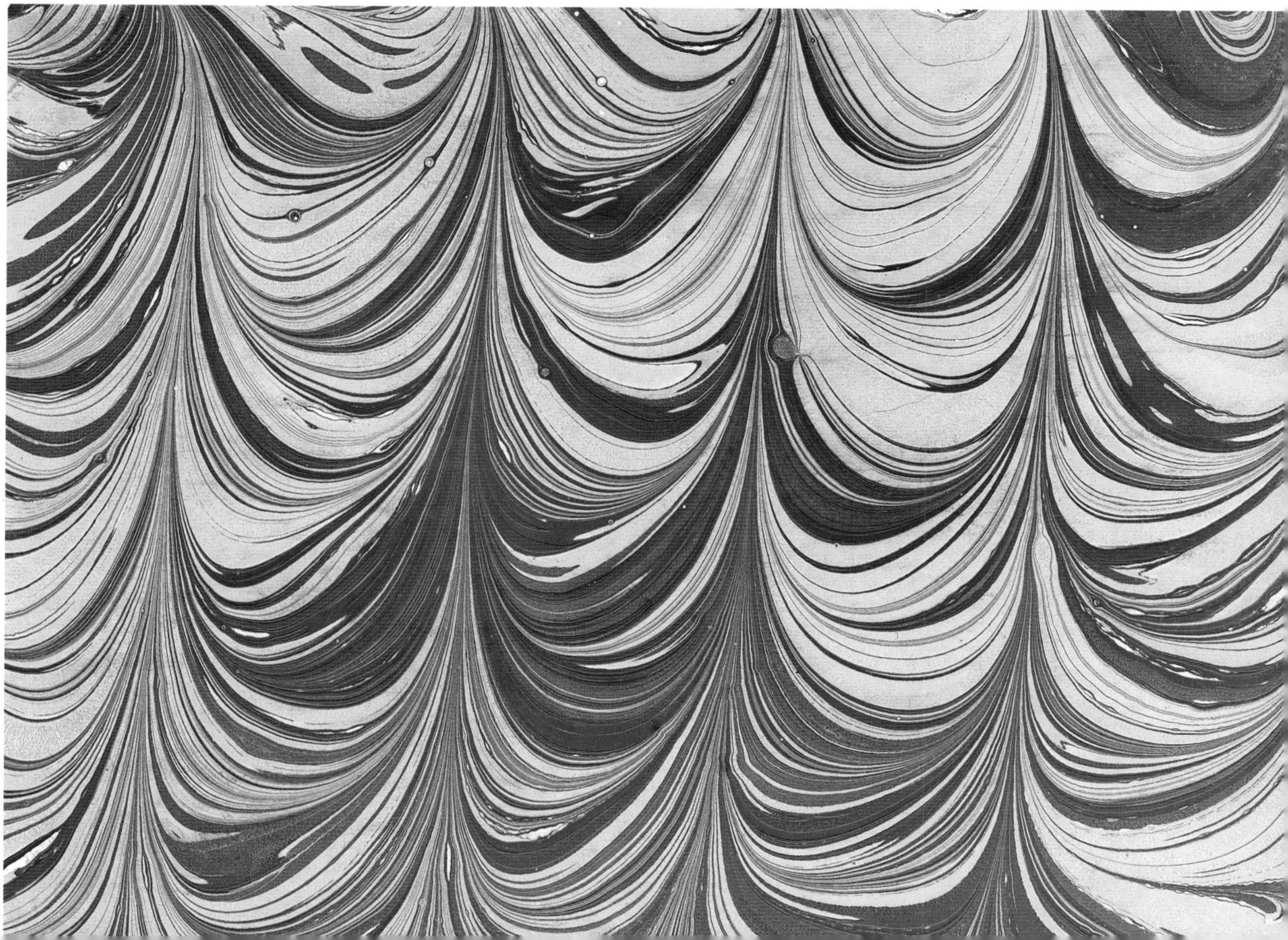

Nonpareil

$\int$ tart with the Back and Forth pattern, as described. Then go over this design using a marbling comb or rake. The teeth on your marbling comb should be between 1/4" and 1/2" apart, and the marbling comb should stretch all the way across the horizontal length of your tray. Insert your comb only through the surface paint—about 1/4" deep—and pull it toward you with a slow and steady hand.

Remember that when using a marbling comb or rake, you must always drag it *against* the pattern of lines. If you have a Back and Forth pattern which ends horizontally, then your comb should be pulled toward you vertically.

AVOID OVERMANIPULATING!

It is precisely for a design such as Nonpareil that you must remember the warning not to overmanipulate. Do not use the comb more than once or you will start to lose the desired delicate look. It is always tempting to keep on playing with the comb and the stylus, but learn when to quit. As already noted, many good, clear designs have been ruined by adding "just one more" stroke. You can only draw the paint out so many times before the tiny lines start to break apart and the colors lose their clarity.

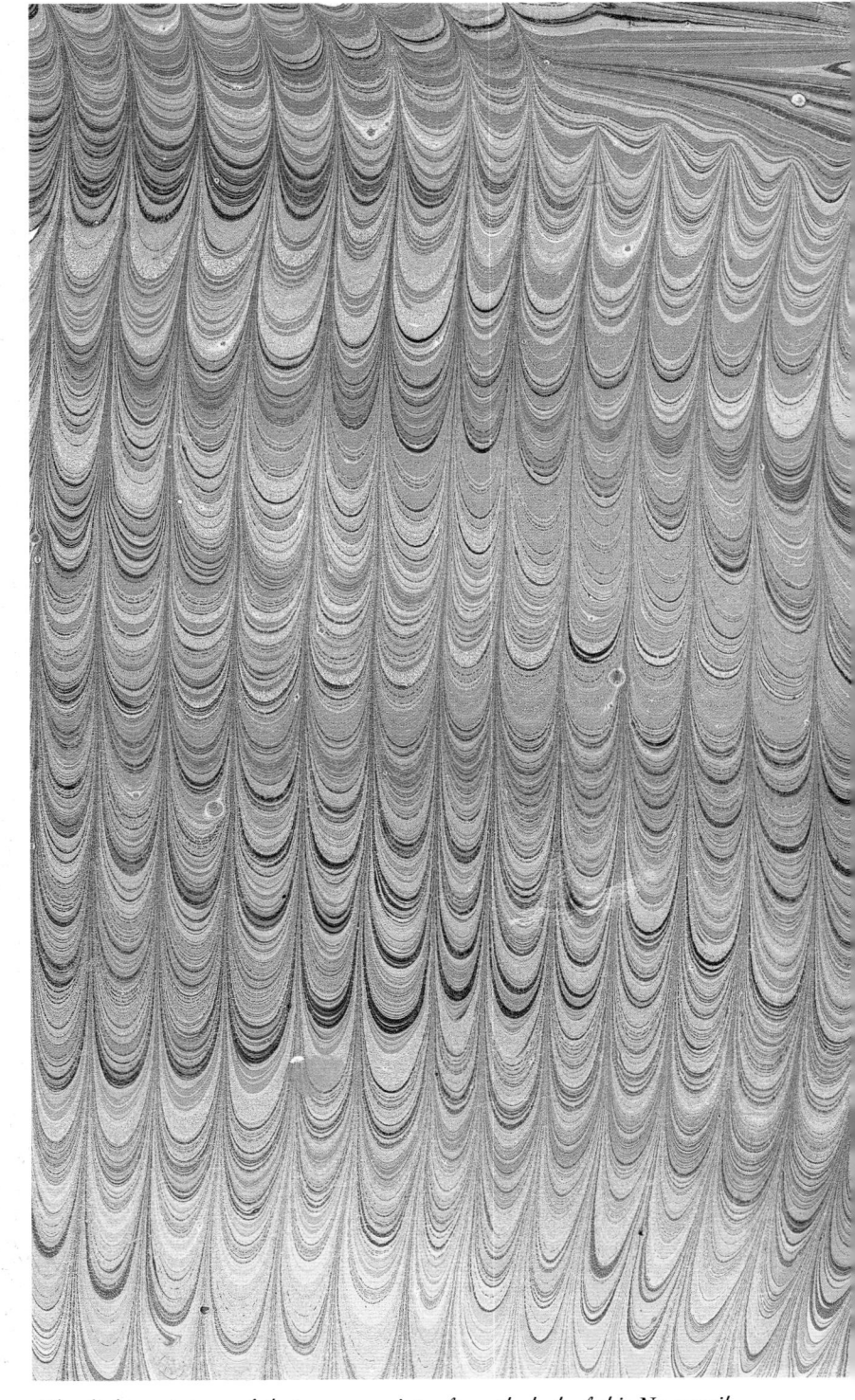

The slight graininess of the tempera paint softens the look of this Nonpareil.

Start with the Back and Forth pattern.

Remember to pull against the pattern of lines. The Nonpareil lines may be made straight or with a slight wave.

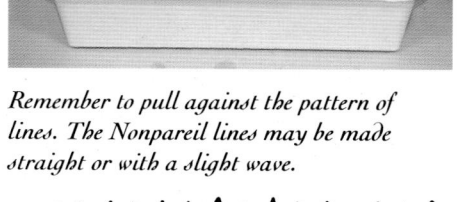

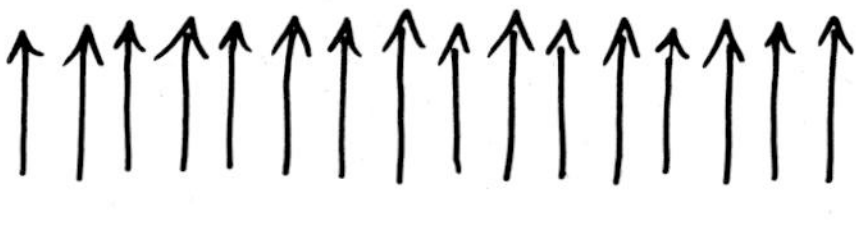

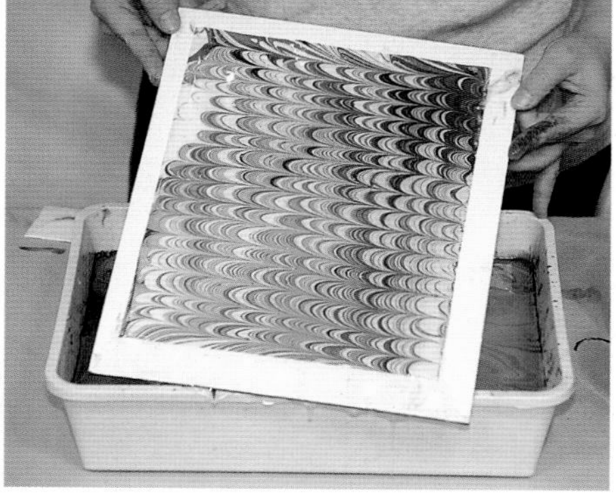

This pattern is a classic of bookbinding.

This Nonpareil was given a slight wave.

The Peacock, or Bouquet

Follow the directions for the Nonpareil pattern, being careful to create an orderly vertical pattern and making sure that when you use the comb you pull from the top of the tray toward you. Next, go over this design with your stylus, always dragging the tool toward you, following the guide shown here. You should be creating a series of reverse squiggles which will create a series of fan-shaped designs.

The Peacock is most effective when the colors change from one side of the paper to the other.

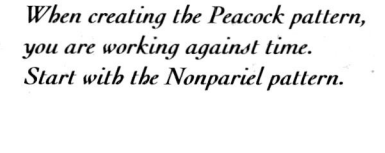

When creating the Peacock pattern, you are working against time. Start with the Nonpariel pattern.

Pull toward you with the stylus.

This Peacock design radiates color.

French Snail

Follow the directions for creating the Nonpareil. Then use your stylus as illustrated to create this snail-shell motif. This pattern is very old and is also called the Antique Dutch and the Curlicue.

If you notice raggedy, broken, or granular lines, or spotty and granular-looking paint aggregations, you are probably working too slowly. You must work quickly in laying down your paints and in creating your combed designs. Finish up within two to three minutes, for your paints will continue to spread and react the longer they sit on the surface. After about three minutes, they will begin to break down, create uneven looks, and lose detail.

Avoid using old paints which have been sitting for months or old size which may be too thin.

Size that is too warm, or paints and size which are at quite different temperatures, can cause problems. For dealing with specific problems that may turn up, you can refer to the "Technical Problems", the next section of the book, beginning on page 97.

This example shows a very regular pattern, but you can have great fun exploring the variations on the curlicue design you draw in the paint.

Here, the French Snail pattern is finished up.

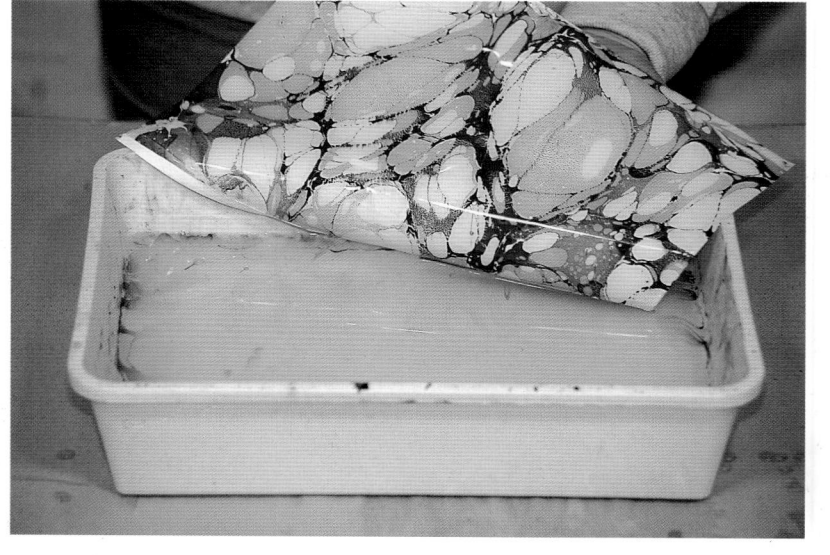

After about three minutes, the paints begin to get granular and spotty (as here), so always work quickly to finish up your design.

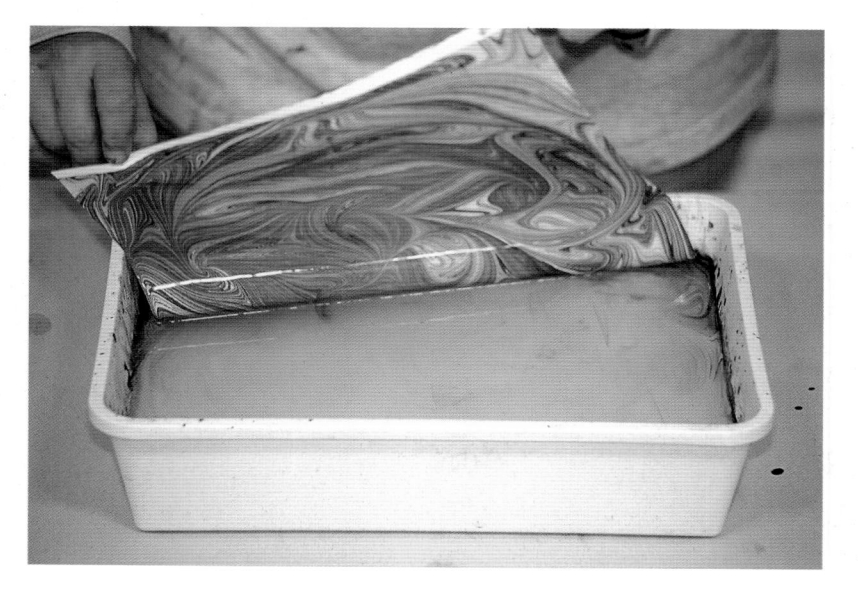

This muddy-looking sheet is the result of overmanipulation of the paints.

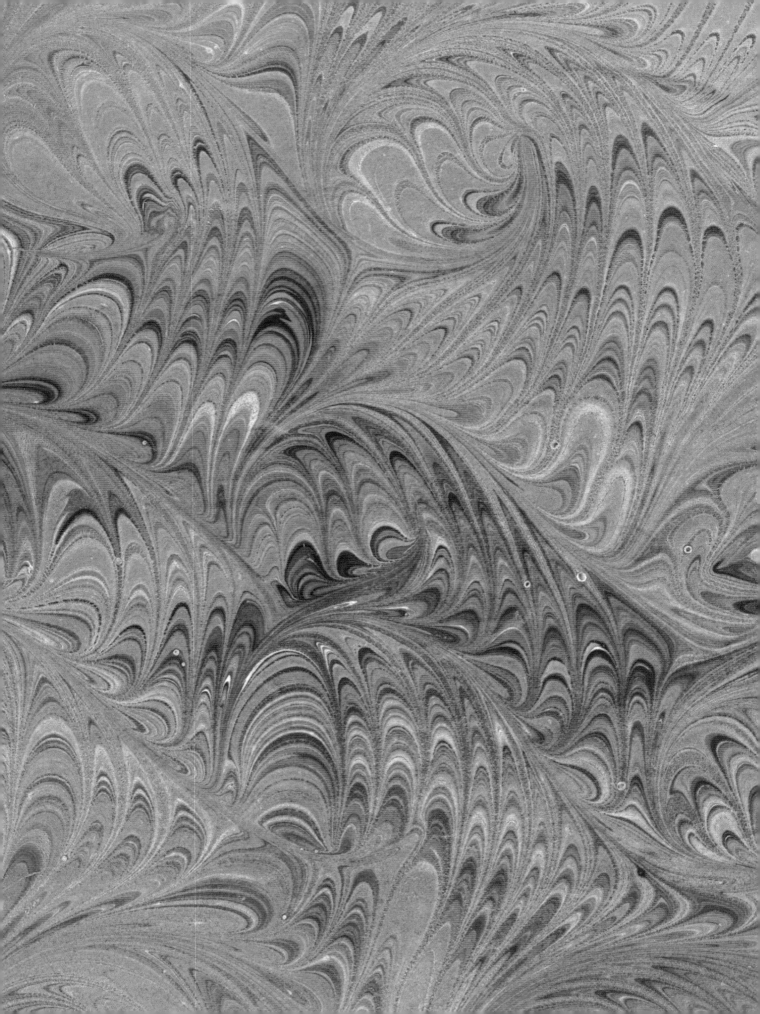

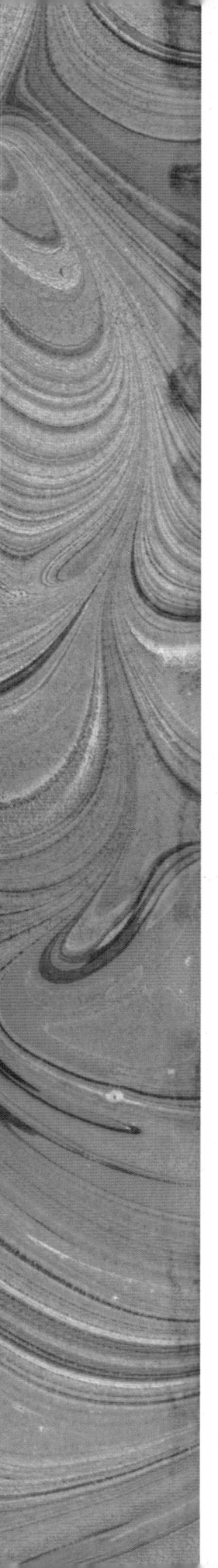

TECHNICAL PROBLEMS

No matter what technique or combination of materials you are using, you will probably run into problems on occasion—large or small white spots, white streaks, paint clumps, and so on. The following is a troubleshooting guide for you to use when those "glitches" occur.

If all else fails look for environmental factors which frequently are the culprit: extremely hard water, or temperature differences between the paints and size (should all be room temperature), too much dust (which causes spots), or any foreign matter, such as traces of oil (which may be in your tray, your mixing cups, or on your tools).

∧ *The raggedy lines in this Peacock pattern were caused by working too slowly.*

< *Know when to quit and you'll avoid this fractured look.*

97

Size and Paint Problems

There are several factors concerning your size that can interfere with the spreading action of your paints. Here are some likely problems and suggested solutions.

SINKING PAINT

Your technique of applying paint to the size may be making your paints break through the surface and sink. *Throwing* your paints onto the base surface is too forceful; you must tap your whisk gently on your finger. *Squirting* your paints on with an eyedropper also forces paint through the surface. Squeeze extremely slowly when using an eyedropper, letting droplet by droplet out—better yet, use a straw. Finally, *overloading* your surface with too much paint is a common occurrence with enthusiastic beginners. A good rule of thumb is to stop applying paints when you notice that the droplets are slowly spreading. If you are using a broom corn whisk, keep your hands moving across the tray continually. This is very important if you are to avoid a paint pile-up in one area and, again, sinking.

FILMY SURFACE

The size surface will commonly have some bubbles, and we have seen how to skim these off. But if you skim off your size twice before beginning and frequently as you go, you will remove not only bubbles, but also impurities which have settled on the surface from the air.

The surface of the size also

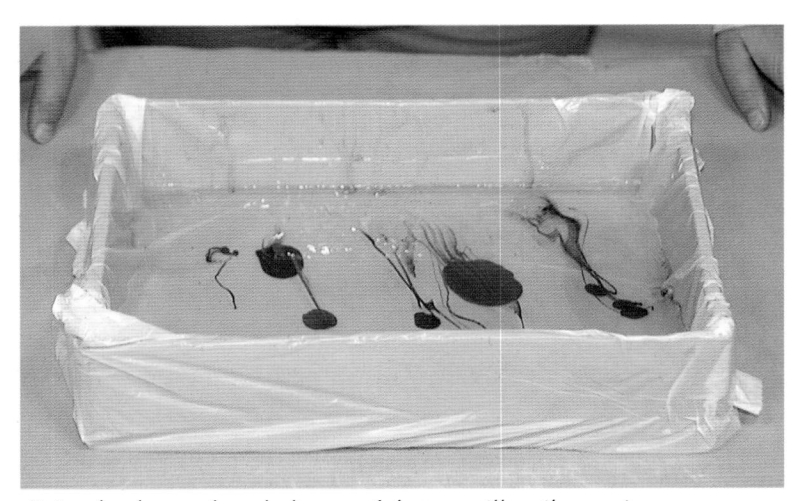

Paint that has sunk to the bottom of the tray will spoil your size.

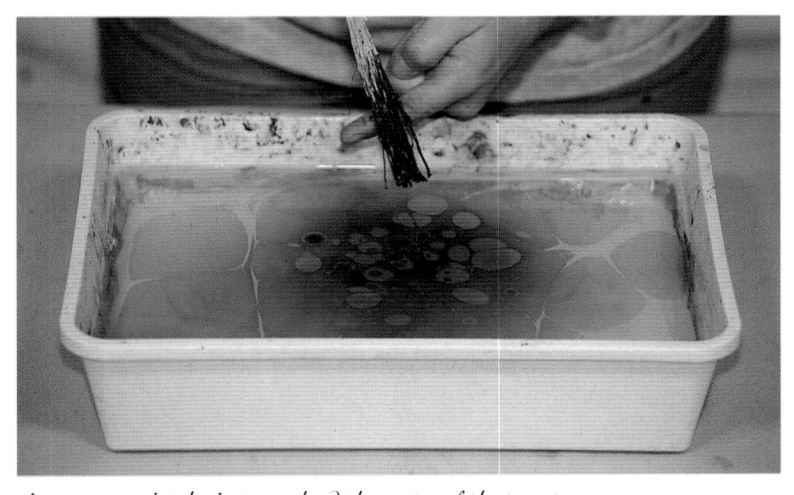

A common mistake is to overload the center of the tray with too much paint. It has nowhere to go but down.

changes: after only five or ten minutes, your size will develop a thin skin on it, due to evaporation. Moreover, residual paint can creep in from all sides of your tray between the marbling of sheets.

In order to skim off your size most efficiently, lay down a sheet of newspaper that fits right up to the edges, lift it up, and throw it away. Many marblers simply scrape any residual paint off to one side, but it will usually creep right back in.

DIRTY SIZE

It is normal for a few drops of paint to sink to the bottom of your tray,

Murkiness like this will interfere with your patterns.

Leftover deposits of paint are barely visible as they creep in from the sides of the tray. Remove the creeping residual paint before printing a new sheet.

even if you are being extremely careful. They will not be a problem as long as they stay there, since the only thing that matters is what is floating on the surface. However, if you have a lot of paint sinking, it will inevitably become mixed up in the size and foul the entire batch from top to bottom. No amount of skimming will help. If your size appears cloudy or gray, throw it all out and start again.

TEMPERATURE DIFFERENCE

If you are getting strange irregular shapes, such as iceberg and star shapes, or if there is virtually no spreading action, check to make sure that your size and paints are all at room temperature. Actually, your size should feel distinctly cold to the touch.

SOME REMINDERS

Remember the following basics:

● The thicker the size, the less the spread of your paints, and the greater your control. If you prefer small, tight patterns, go this route.

● The thinner your size—the more watered down it is—the more spread you will have, for you have freed up the surface tension. You can work much more quickly then and will get wonderful loose and organic designs.

● Never *throw* or *squirt* your paints onto the size surface with too much force, and do not *overload* your surface with too much paint. These actions will cause paint to sink. Stop applying paints when you notice that the droplets are slowly spreading.

● If you are using a broom corn whisk, keep your hands moving across the tray continually to avoid a paint pile-up in one area or a sinking of paint.

● If you do find that your paints are sinking, try a thicker size or thinner paints. Use a more delicate hand as you create a pattern with your stylus.

● If your paints are floating but not spreading effectively, thin down your size slightly or add a few drops of spreading medium to your paints.

● In making a good-looking finished sheet, avoid applying too much color, for this will not only cause paint sinkage and a murky tray but a muddled design as well (see page 100).

Muddled Design

Lack of definition, or just a dull or muddled look, in your design could be caused by overmanipulation of the paint; too much paint; a size that has been discolored with paint; or a lack of color contrast. You can only draw out tiny lines of paint about four or five times before they start to break down. Also, if you leave your paints standing on the size too long, they will start to get grainy. Plan on applying your paints and creating your pattern within three to four minutes.

The effects of size that is not clean will be reflected in your sheet. And rethinking your palette may be the answer; contrasting colors are often the key to a vibrant design.

Lack of definition.

White Areas

Large, irregularly shaped white areas are usually caused by air trapped underneath the paper as you lay it down. Be sure not to "drop" the paper onto the surface. Small white areas may be touched up after the sheet is dry.

Large, irregularly shaped white area.

Smaller white spots.

White Spots

Smaller white spots are usually caused by bubbles on the surface of the size. Before you put down any paint, look for them and prick them, or, if they are numerous, scrape them against the edge of the tray. If the spots interfere with your finished design, use watercolor to touch them up.

White, streaky lines.

White Streaks

White, streaky-looking lines are frequently caused by hesitating when laying down the paper. Lay down your sheet with one smooth motion, keeping your hands steady.

Faded Patches

Paints fade out in places because they are washed away in the rinsing process. You must either rinse more delicately (mainly by turning down the water pressure) or begin treating your papers with a mordant.

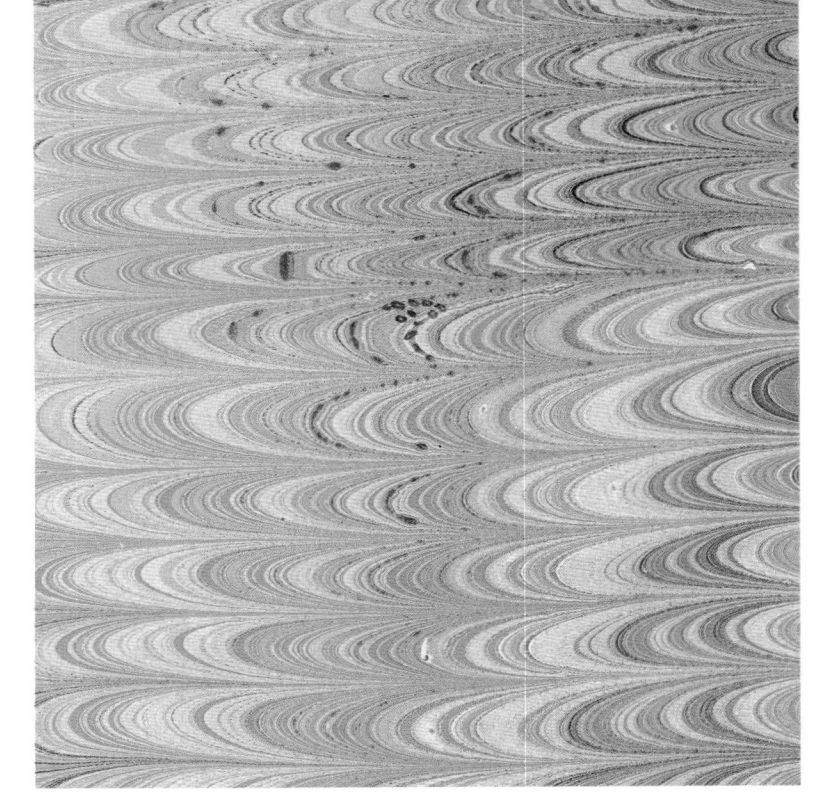

Paints disappear in the rinsing.

Odd Shapes

Star or iceberg shapes are usually caused by a too-warm size. Your size should be distinctly cold to the touch. You should also check for the possibility of a foreign substance in your paints.

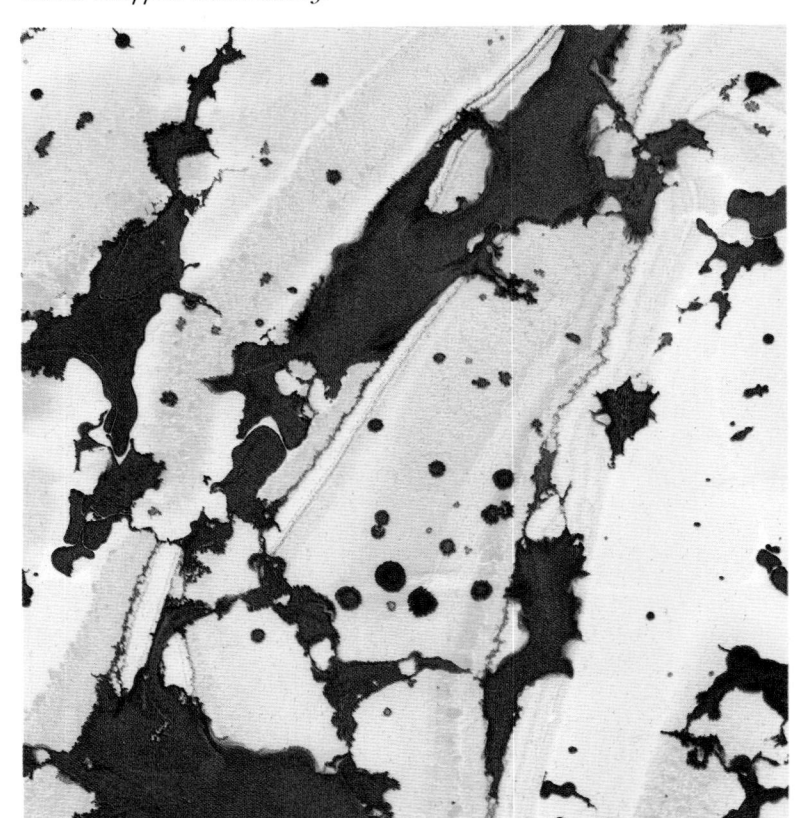

Stars and icebergs.

"Eyes" of Color

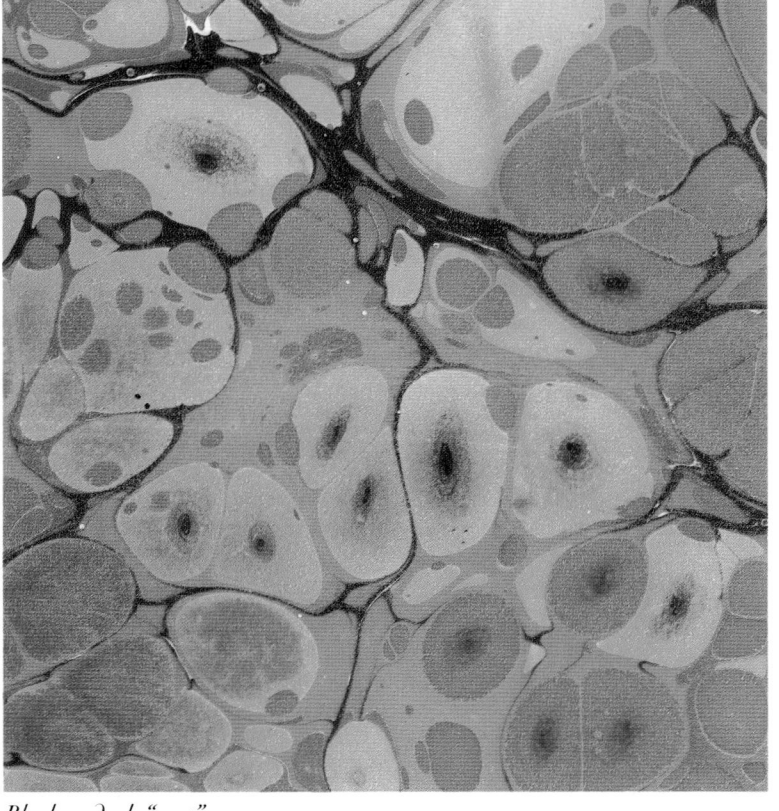

Black or dark "eyes".

In the center of your pools of color sometimes spots, or "eyes," can form that fail to disperse. These can sometimes be prevented by adding a tiny amount of spreading medium. You can also pick them up, along with other surface flaws, with a small paper tab.

Paint Clumps

Spotty clumps of paint.

Spotty clumps of paint often appear in the design when the paints have been whipped or stirred up too vigorously in their containers. A froth results and will gum up your design with ugly and ragged clumps which appear on your finished sheet.

SPECIAL TECHNIQUES

Once you have mastered all the basic and traditional patterns, you may want to go further and test your own ideas for obtaining amazing special effects. The Spanish Wave pattern, for instance, is an astonishing variation on the Turkish Stone or other pattern achieved by moving the paper on the surface of the size. Flower motifs, on the other hand, are created by using the stylus to "draw" petals and leaves in the floating paint. You can similarly draw other motifs that intrigue you. Other applications demonstrated in the next few pages include marbling borders, marbling with stencils and colored paper, vignetting, and marbling objects. These are techniques to spark any marbler's imagination.

∧ *Marbling with tempera using a bottled starch creates a furry line and a soft look.*

< *This eerie landscape by Olaf resulted from a careful arrangement of colors.
A sprinkling of thinned spreading agent created the snow effect.*

Spanish Wave

For a truly exquisite pattern, create a Turkish Stone with a sumptuous veining. The trick is to lay your paper down more slowly than usual starting from one corner of the sheet.

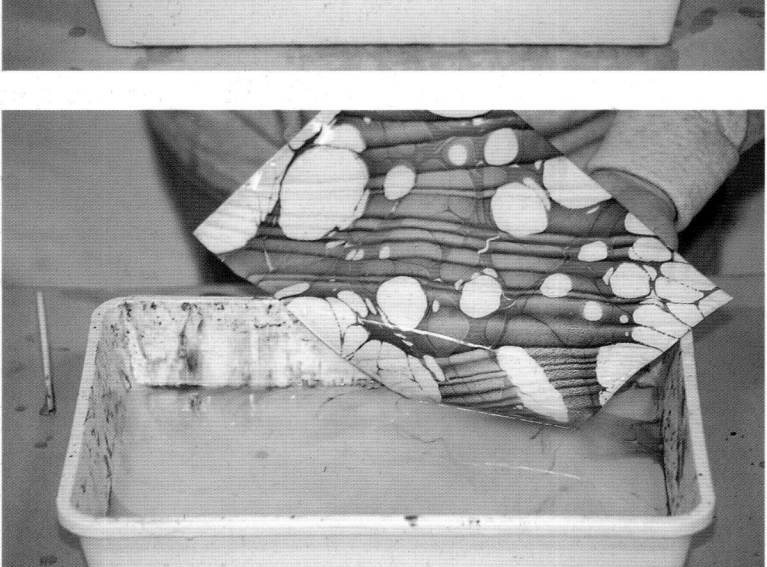

At the same time, shift the paper back and forth. To allow for the back and forth movement of the sheet, have a 1" leeway all around it.

Nothing quite compares with the three-dimensional wave illusion caused by your hand motion.

> The Spanish Wave look can give the impression of a watery stream bed.

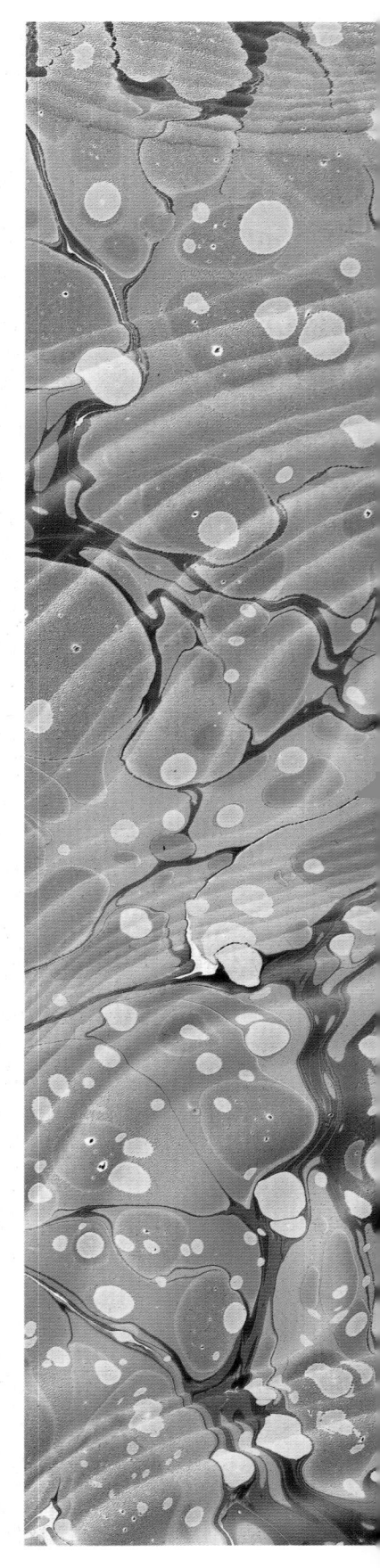

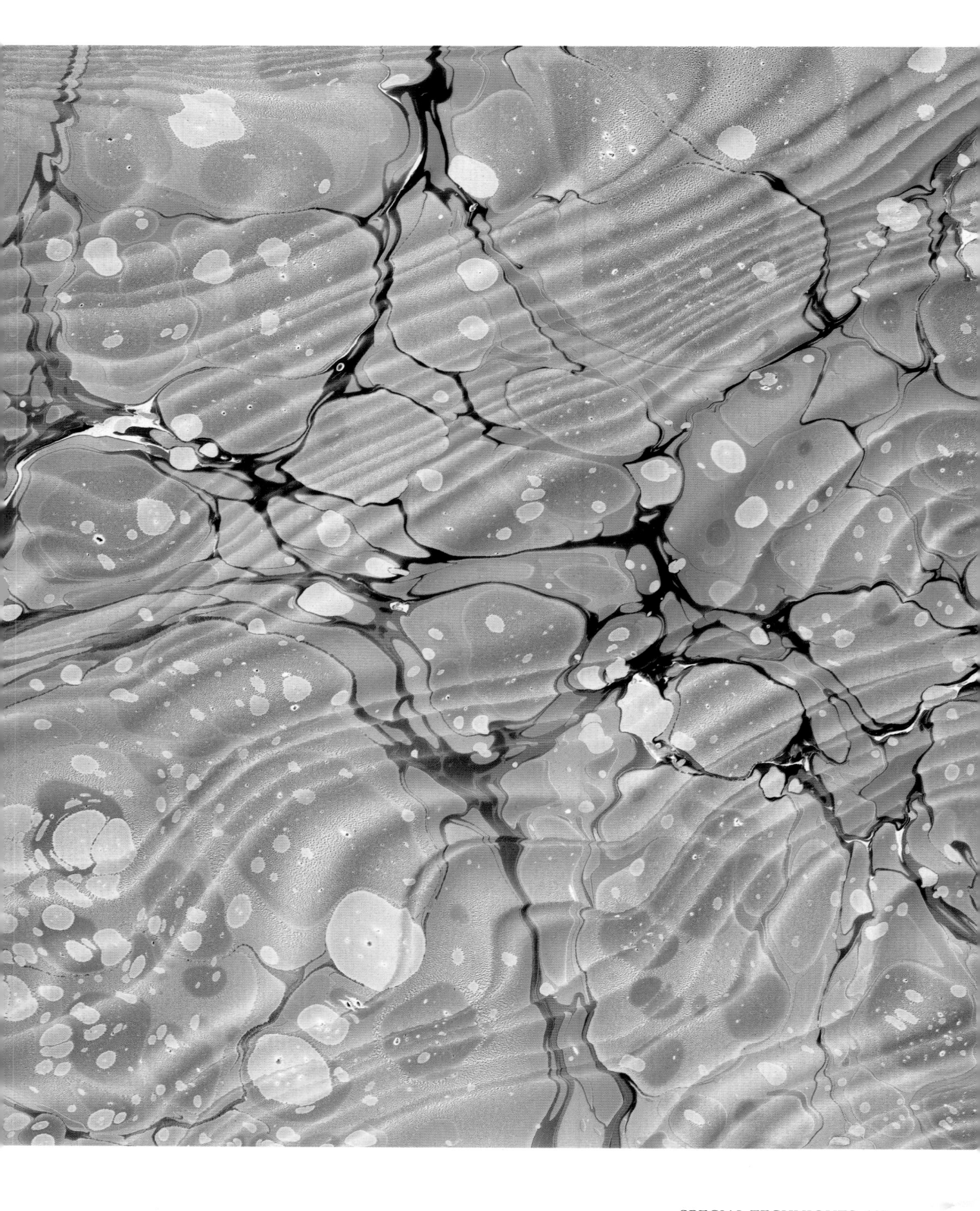

Flower Marbling

> The marbled flower is a
traditional Turkish motif.

Use an eyedropper or straw to deposit a single drop
of paint onto the surface.

After it has completely dispersed,
add a contrasting drop of paint.

Concentric rings of color develop.

You can easily coax the rings of color into bloom
with a fine-pointed stylus.

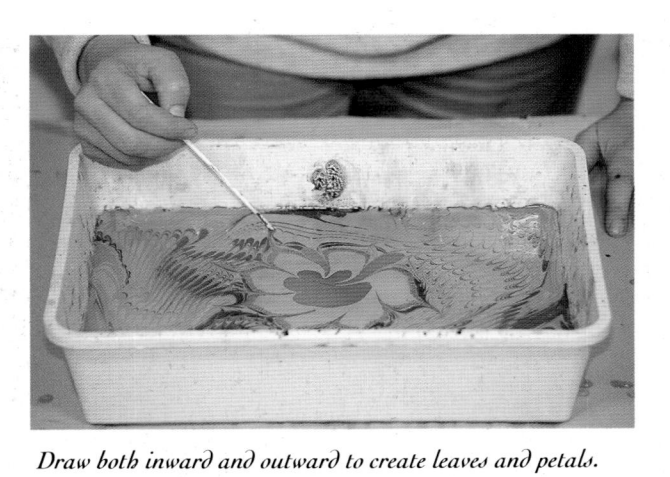

Draw both inward and outward to create leaves and petals.

The same technique may be used to create
birds and other figures.

Marbled Borders

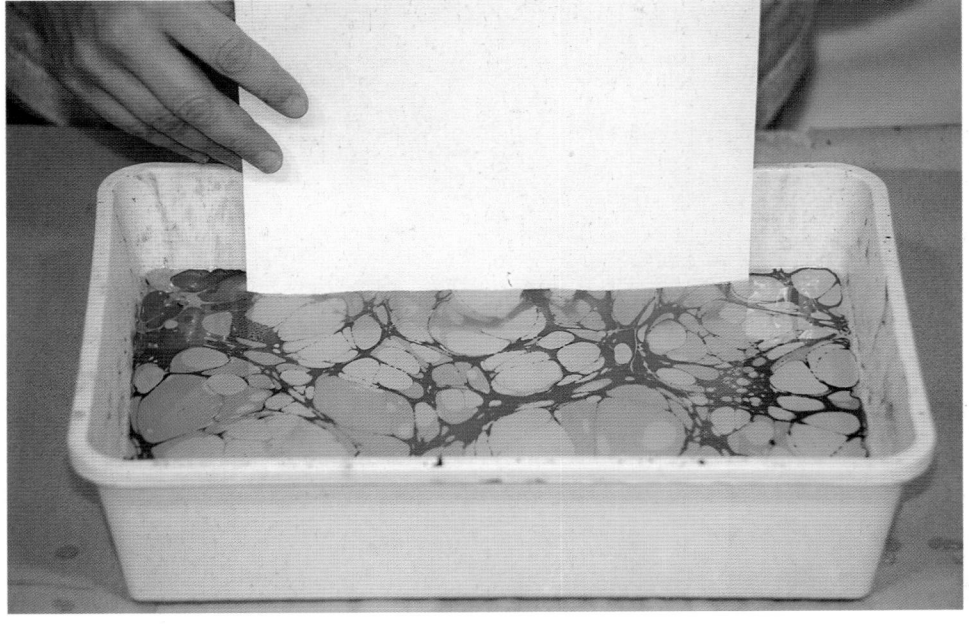

Dip one end of your paper about an inch into the size.

∨ You can dip two or all four sides to create a border on stationery and calligraphy pieces.

Marbling on Colored Paper

Using a colored paper will give you rich hues.

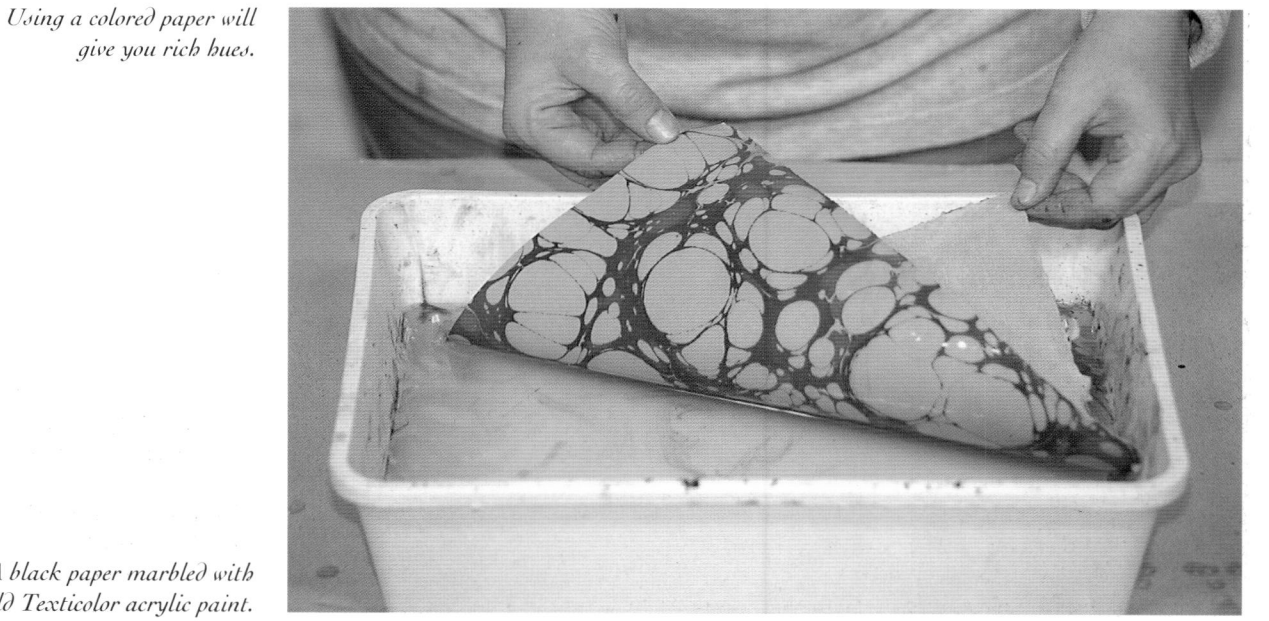

∨ *A black paper marbled with gold Texticolor acrylic paint.*

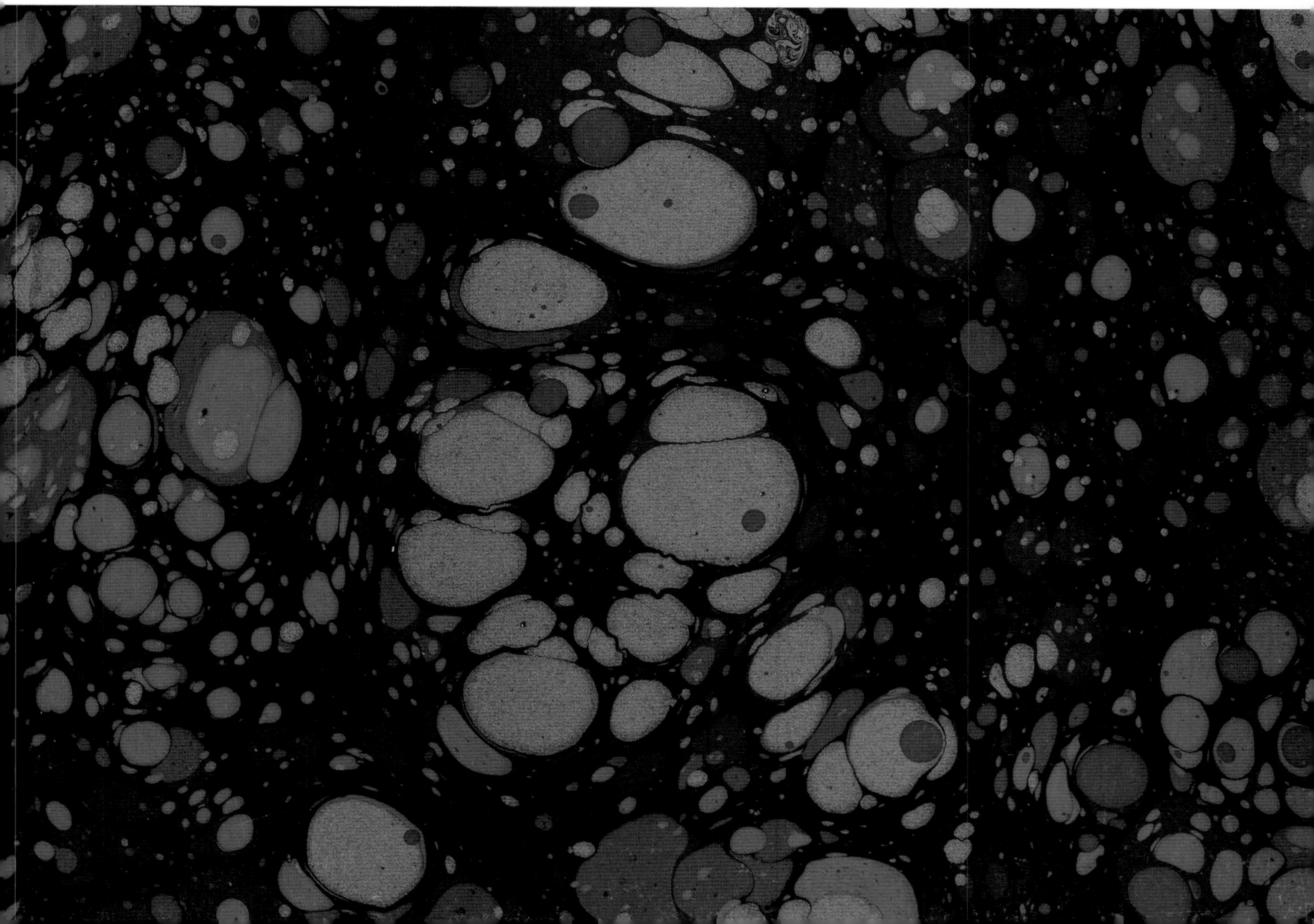

Stencil Marbling

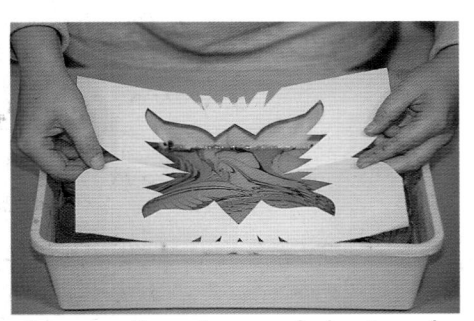

Cut a stencil out of paper and place it gently on the surface.

Quickly place a sheet of marbling paper on top of the stencil.

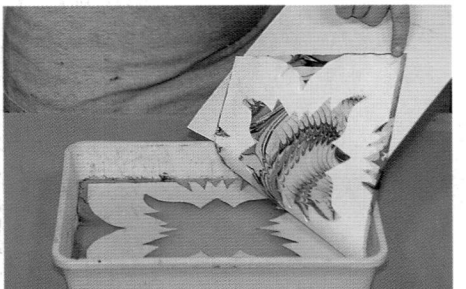

Peel off the stencil-marbled sheet and rinse immediately.

Both the stencil and marbled sheet are finished pieces.

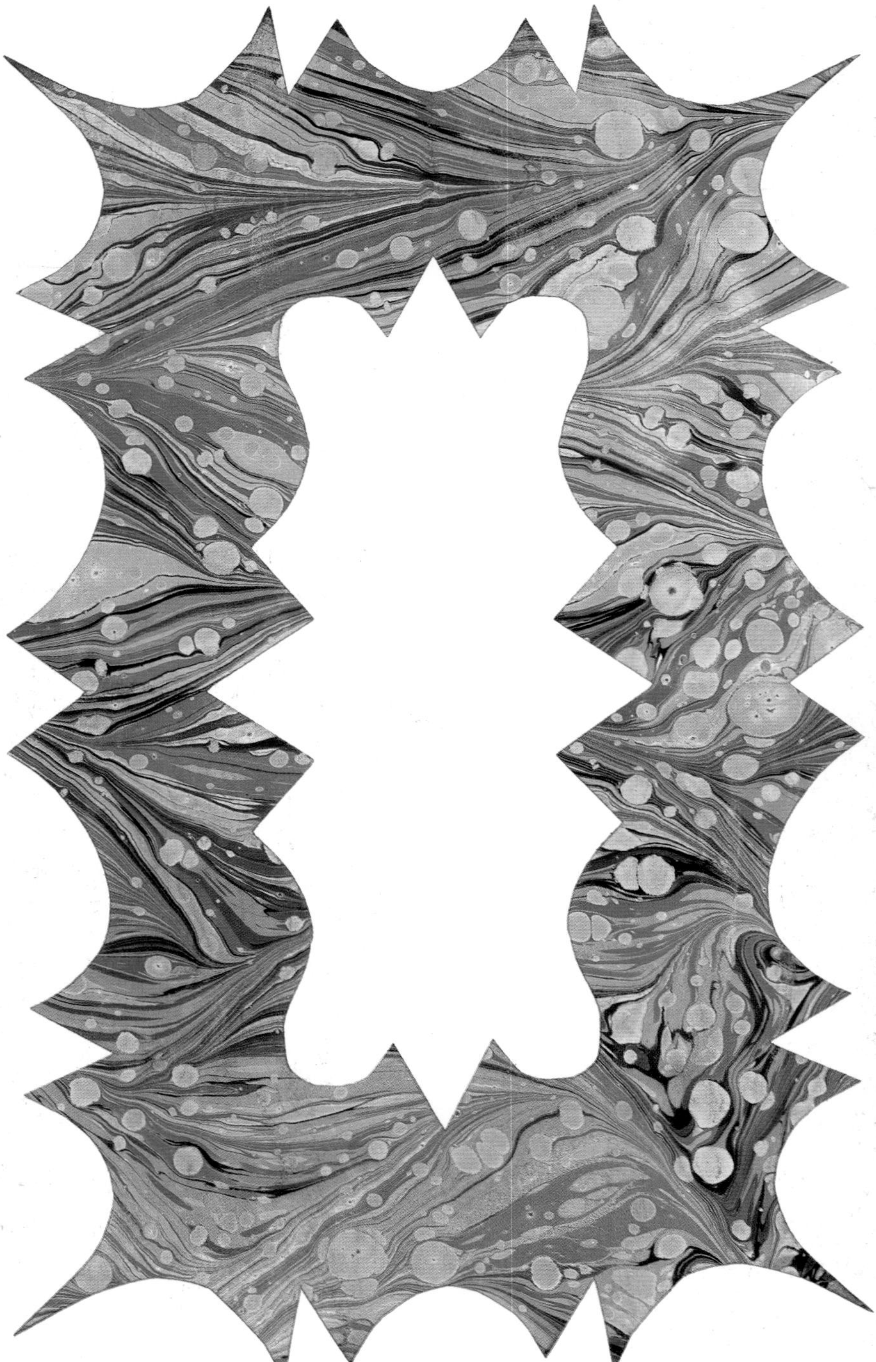

Both positive (above) and negative (right) stencils can be used.

Fade-outs and Vignettes

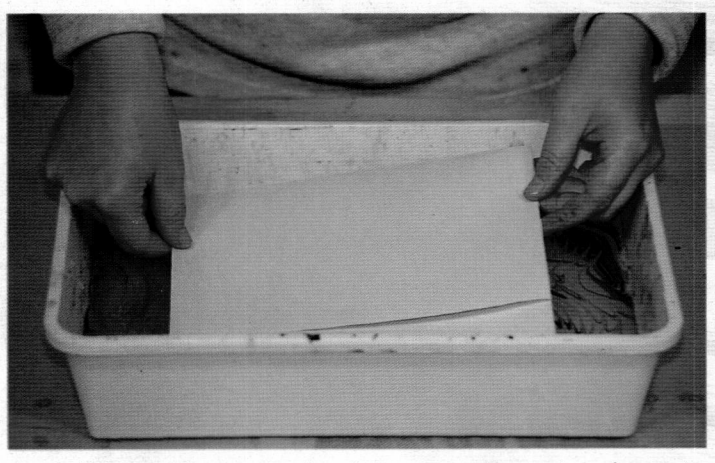

In the floating paint, create a free-form pattern. Lay a piece of paper in the very center of it, then pick it up. Let the leftover paints creep in toward the blank center for a few seconds, then pick up the remaining design with a new sheet.

The interesting result is a design that fades into a white center, giving you a soft border all around.

Marbling Objects

Objects such as this egg must be coated with an acrylic gesso before marbling.

The egg is "rolled" across the size surface while suspended on a wire. You can also carefully dip the object.

In the case of a marbled object, you do not rinse it. Let it dry and finish it with a clear waterproof coating.

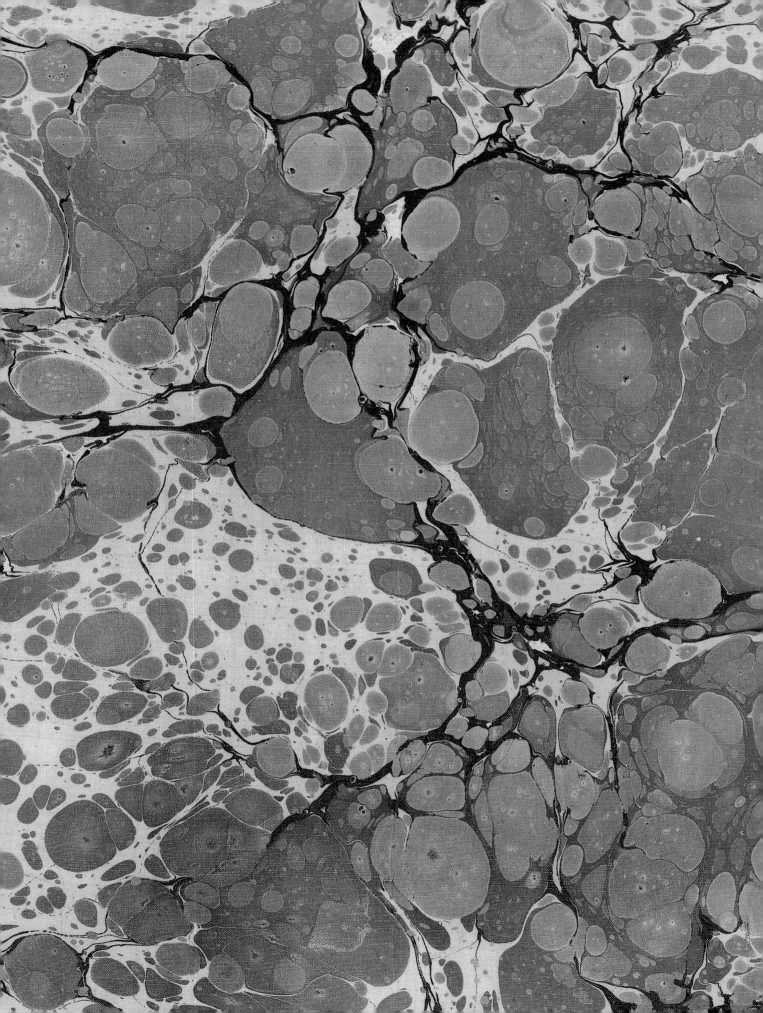

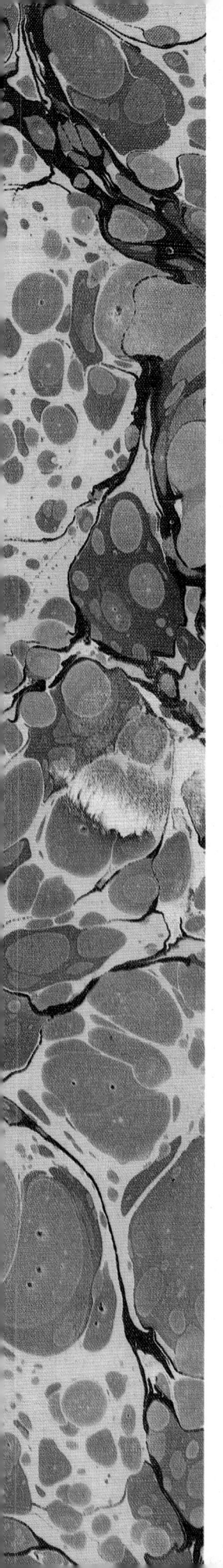

MARBLING ON FABRIC

Marbling on fabric yields especially beautiful results on shimmering, smooth silk. When making your patterns for fabrics, be resourceful; my rule of thumb is "the bolder the better." Marbling on fabric presents few difficulties for anyone who has mastered the basics of marbling on paper. You are somewhat limited to acrylics in your choice of paints, however. Oil paints, water-based gouache paints, and tempera paints simply will not work on fabrics. However, any type of size medium will work just fine, although methocel seems to rinse out of the fabric more easily.

∧ *Four hands are needed to lay down a large piece of silk fabric.*

< *A stone pattern marbled on a heavy cream-colored silk.*

There are only two paints currently on the market which I would highly recommend for fabric. The first is Portfolio, a ready-mixed marbling paint with excellent adhesion, the second is Texticolor Opaque, imported from France. Texticolor Opaque was formulated for use on fabrics. These particular types of acrylic paint are permanent when heat-set on fabric and require little or no paint additives in the way of a spreading medium. You will simply need to mix up your colors and thin them with water until they are able to float and spread on the surface of your size. A small amount of Winsor & Newton acrylic flow agent may be helpful.

When choosing a fabric, look for a smooth finish and a tight weave that will allow the maximum amount of detail to be transferred. Extremely nubbly and loosely woven fabrics such as canvas, muslin, or raw silk will give you a somewhat raggedy version of your marbled design. But you can marble on almost any fabric, including polyesters. Your best effects, however, will always be on silk. The fluidity and luminosity of silk seems to be perfectly complemented by marbled designs.

It is advisable that you wash and dry the fabric before you begin in order to remove any starchy material that has been put on it by the manufacturer. After your fabric is clean, you must treat it with an alum mordant (see page 48) as you would with paper. This acts to chemically bond the marbling paints into the fibers of the fabric. Create the alum solution as for paper (about one tablespoon of aluminum sulphate per cup of hot water), and then dip your fabric

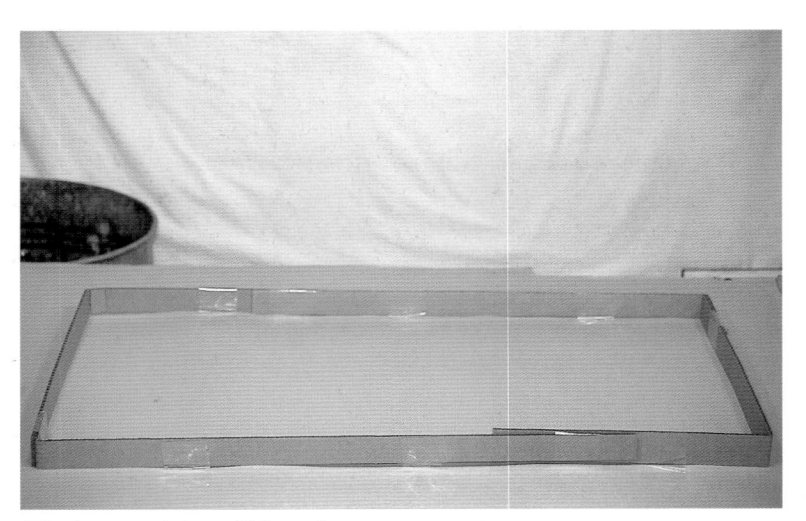

The framework is taped into place.

Here, plastic sheeting has been taped down. There is no need to use more than a 3/4" deep size unless you are doing multiple pieces of fabric.

Work quickly to cover this large area.

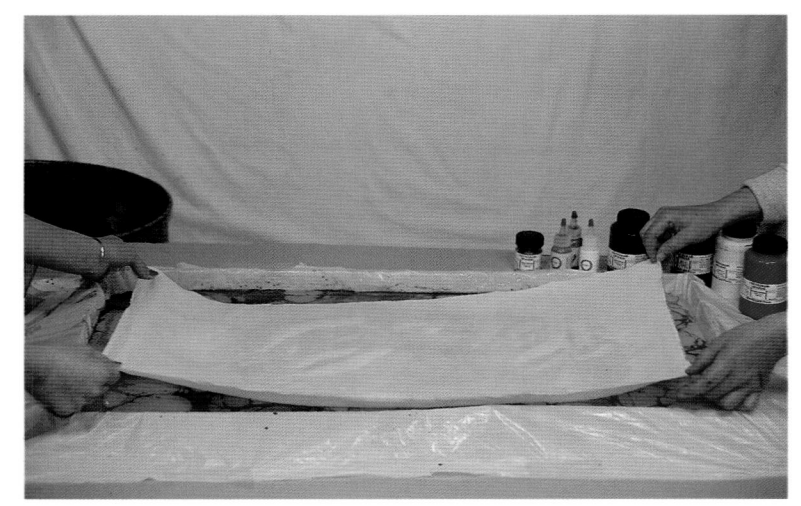

Four hands are needed to lay down a large piece. Air bubbles will gently fall by themselves.

Handle the wet fabric very gently

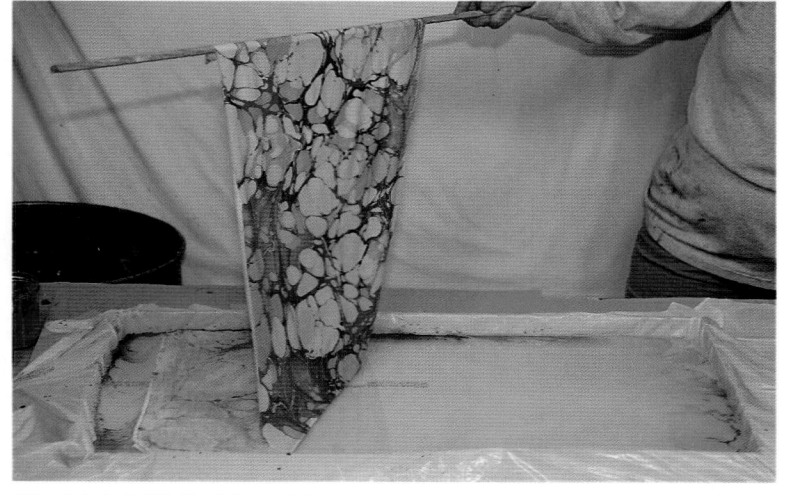

The fabric is lifted with a stick.

piece into the solution until it is soaked through. Lift it up and drape it over a line until it is dry. If it appears to be somewhat wrinkled, run a warm iron over it.

You may marble on any shape or size of fabric you care to use. If you are going to create a marbled silk scarf or a tie, you should marble on a piece of yardage of the fabric, not just the small piece necessary, before you sew it up. Otherwise you will not have a clean-looking finished piece.

In order to create an inexpensive, impromptu tray for use in any fabric marbling project, first create a framework 1" wider all around than the fabric piece. Use corrugated cardboard which you have cut into 2" strips against the grain (that is, across the lines of corrugation). By cutting it against the grain, you will make it very easy to bend and fold around the corners wherever you wish. Using masking tape, tape the framework down onto your working surface. Line this framework with plastic sheeting, such as a plastic trash bag. If you need an extremely large piece of plastic, you may cut two trash bags apart and tape them together tightly. After you have lined your cardboard framework, tape your plastic sheeting down all the way around so that it will not intrude by falling back down into your size.

This is also very easy to clean up and dispose of, for you can pick up the four corners of your plastic after you have done the marbling, tie them together, and discard the dirty size and leftover cardboard into the trash.

If you are marbling a piece which is 30" square or less, you should have no problem in laying down your fabric by yourself. In some ways, laying down a piece of silk on the marbling surface is easier than laying a sheet of paper, because you will never have to worry about air bubbles being trapped under the surface. On the other hand, you do have to worry about laying your silk down in a way which would result in folds or overlapping. This will interrupt your design, and it will be very difficult for you to repair.

If you are marbling by yourself and have a small project at hand, you may lay the silk down by picking up two corners, lifting it over your marbling tray, and laying it down very slowly, starting at the opposite end of your tray. You will notice that as soon as your silk has touched down at the opposite end, it will be held into place, enabling you to gently lay the remainder of your fabric down.

If you have a large or strangely shaped item, you may need another pair of hands, in which case each person should handle a different end of the fabric piece and, together, lay it very gently down, letting it touch down *in the middle first.*

As soon as the fabric has absorbed the paint—it should take a only few seconds—lift it up and rinse it very carefully in a large tub of warm water. Do not wring, twist, or crumple the fabric while you are rinsing it; simply swish it around very slowly for several minutes until you can feel that most of the size is no longer clinging to the fabric surface. Then grasp two corners and very slowly lift it out, hang it painted side up over a wooden rod of some sort, and let it drip dry.

If you are using Texticolor Opaque or Portfolio, you can easily heat-set your finished piece after it has completely dried. Warm your iron to a medium-heat setting, which is about right for cotton, and iron it gently on both sides. After it has been heat-set, your fabric piece may be washed by hand and air-dried without losing any of its color.

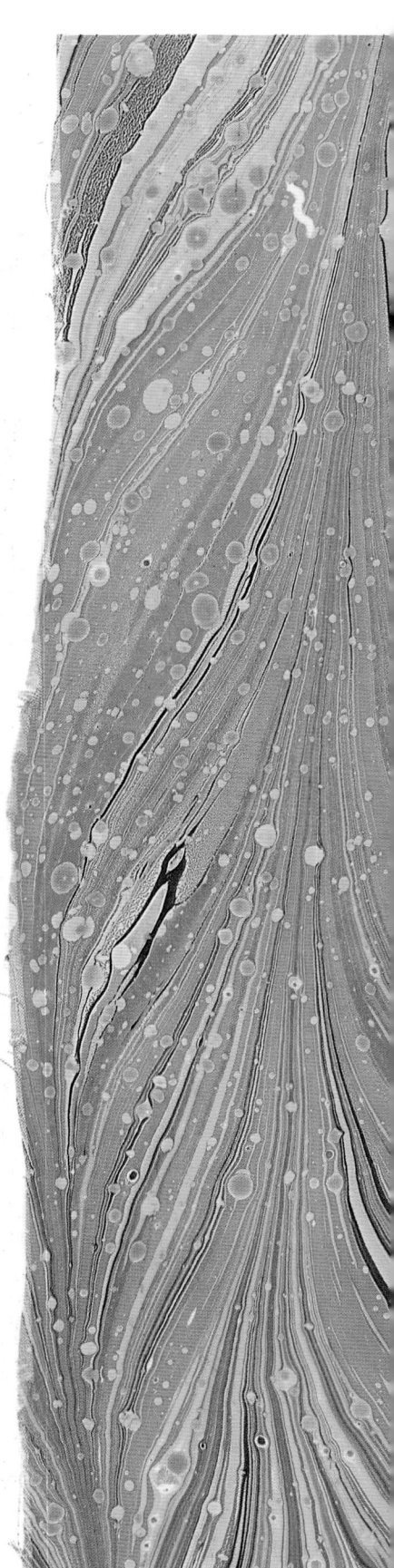

A Back and Forth pattern on Habotai silk.

SUGGESTED PROJECTS

Many people ask what you can do with marbled papers, so I have compiled this section to impart some suggestions: covering boxes, making marbled picture mats, creating book covers and cards. There are other, numerous ways to use your patterned sheets; you will come up with a few on your own. Another project I like to encourage is offering children the opportunity to do marbling. This will often lead to some delightful experiments. The following pages offer just a few ideas to get you started on your creative path.

∧ *This portfolio makes a handsome container for photos, letters, and cards.*
< *Marbling by Monica, age five.*

Marbling with Children

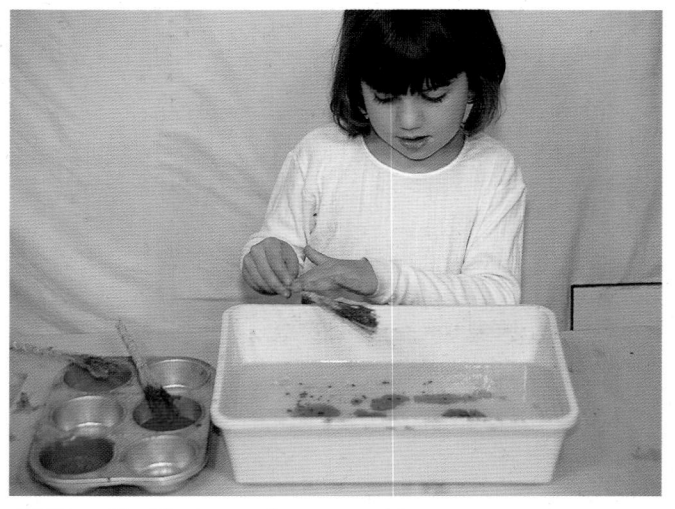

Children like Monica can become marblers. Easy does it on the colors.

Marbling is an art of instant transformation that enchants all ages. Children as young as four years old, with the supervision of an adult, can make beautiful Back and Forth patterns as well as free-form ones. The finished sheets make beautiful gift items, book covers, and cards.

When marbling with children, it is easiest to use the Vano Blue starch, which is ready to use; it may be poured directly into your tray with no preparation whatsoever. Be sure to use a small—child-sized—tray. An 8 1/2 × 11" or 9 × 12" tray is sufficiently large. Use only tempera paints when working with children, for they are the most nontoxic and the easiest to clean up. Mixing your paints in a muffin tin will help to avoid spills. Thin your temperas with water and add a spreading medium drop by drop.

A very good and inexpensive paper to use is manila paper, commonly found in craft, art-supply, and stationery stores and even in discount department stores. Manila paper has a beautiful cream-color and a lot of tooth on the surface to hold onto the paint. You'll have no need to mordant.

Children should be instructed carefully on how much paint to use, and you need to watch to make sure that they do not play too long in creating their designs. Making the design using a stylus or a comb is so much fun that children (as well as adults) have a tendency to get carried away and end up with a confused design. Encourage them to go light on the paints and to keep their design simple. Free-form patterns are especially wonderful for children because it is easy to make one which will have its own special appeal.

A free-form pattern releases the creative impulse.

Taking care with the manila paper, and after only a moment's wait. . . .

Beautiful results and a sense of accomplishment.

Covered Boxes

U se found boxes, such as cigar boxes, or make the box yourself out of sturdy cardboard. I recommend using yellow Glue Sticks for small projects and white library paste, Yes or Tacky brand paste for larger boxes. When applying one of the more fluid pastes, use a small piece of cardboard to apply it in a thin, smooth coating.

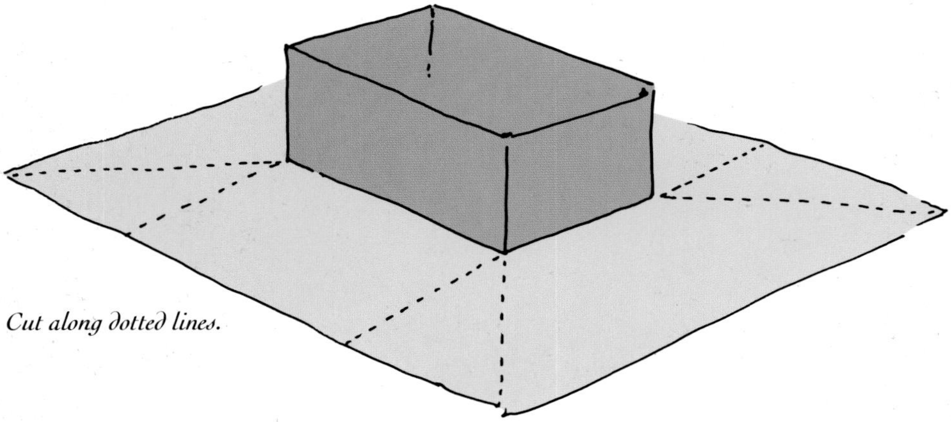

Cut along dotted lines.

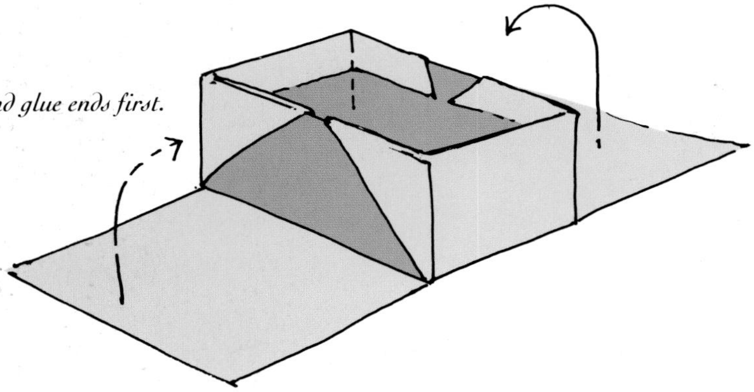

Wrap and glue ends first.

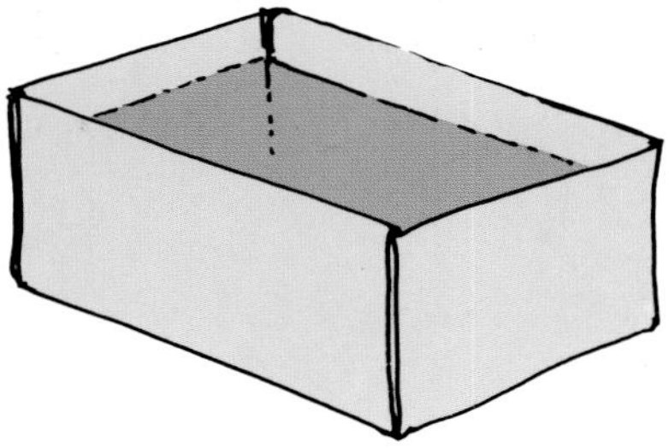

Side pieces cover nicely.

Marbled boxes make wonderful gifts.

Mats for Picture Frames

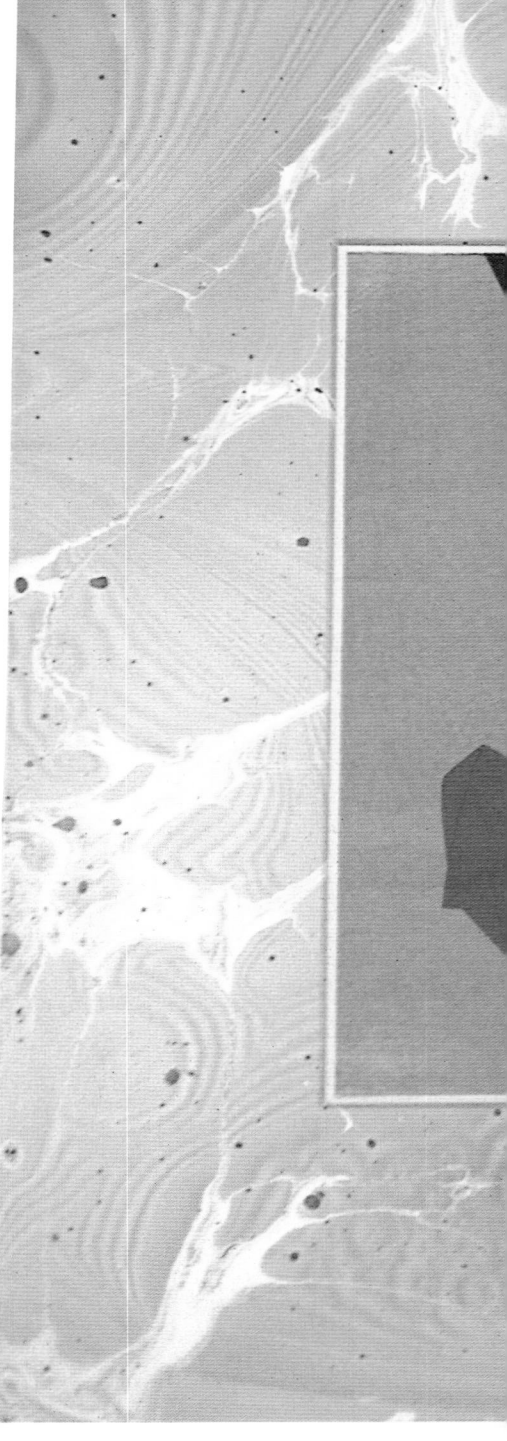

Cover the mat with paper after you have cut the hole. Then cut the marbled paper so that you can wrap around the inner edges and glue it underneath. It is also possible to wrap around the outer edges and to use the finished product as a picture frame and mat all in one.

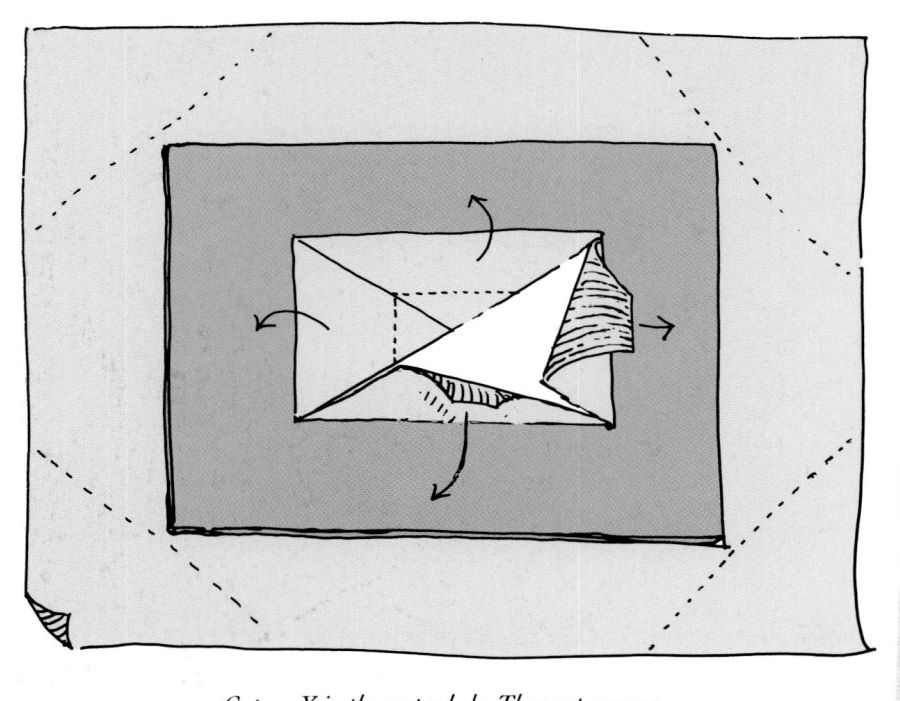

Cut an X in the center hole. Then cut corners on the dotted lines. Wrap the paper around and glue down on the back of the mat.

An important consideration in crafting a picture mat is your choice of colors. Obviously, this application of marbling permits you to tailor the color scheme and the marbled pattern to the picture. Often a muted design will work best and not distract from the image. Here, a perfect harmony was achieved between the art and the custom-made mat.

Bookbinding

Create your own bookbinding design to dress up your paperback books. Cover the book by gluing and wrapping the cover with your paper.

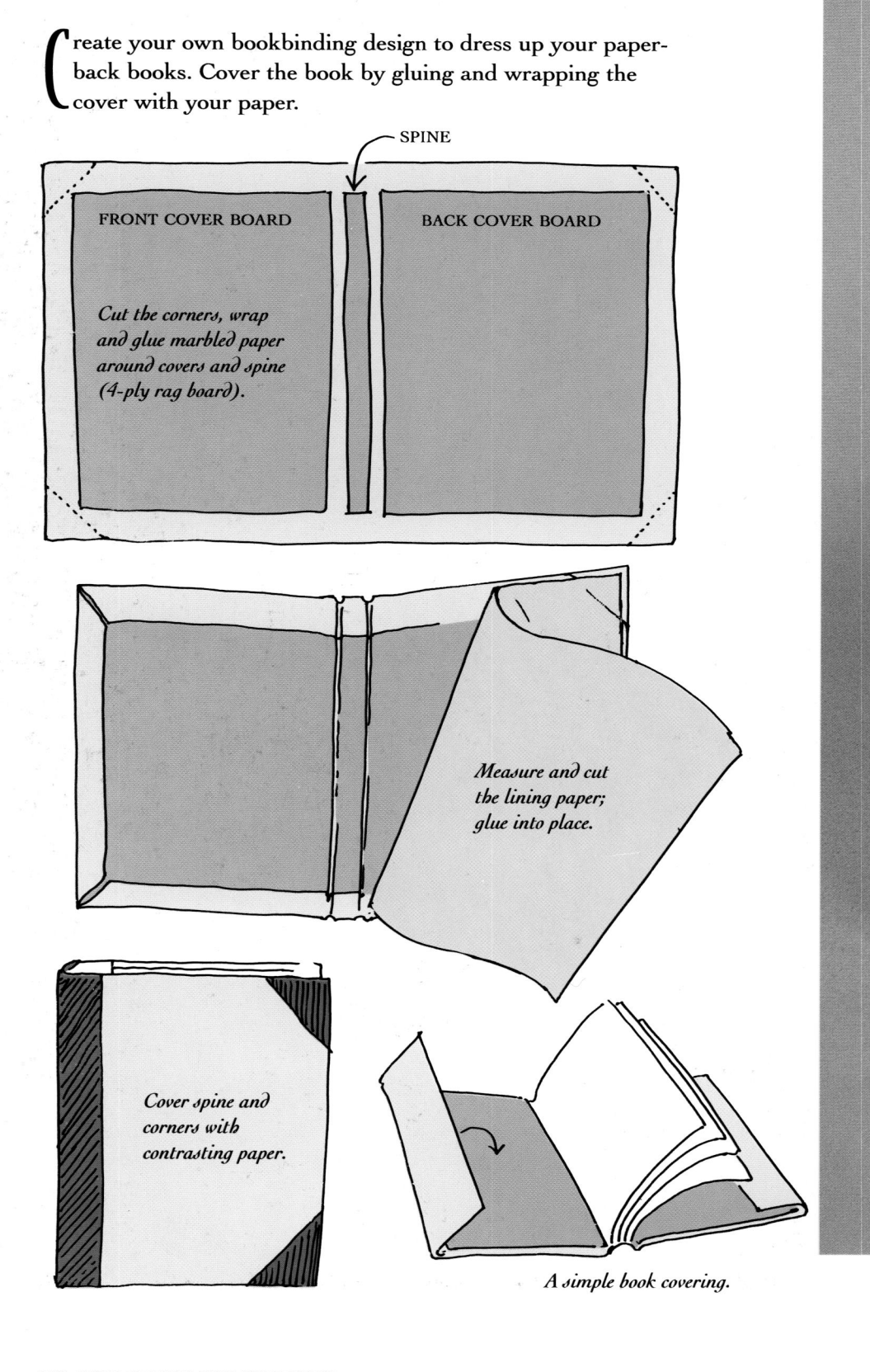

SPINE

FRONT COVER BOARD

BACK COVER BOARD

Cut the corners, wrap and glue marbled paper around covers and spine (4-ply rag board).

Measure and cut the lining paper; glue into place.

Cover spine and corners with contrasting paper.

A simple book covering.

Marbled papers are a natural choice for modern and traditional bindings for books of all kinds.

NOTE BOOK

Greeting Cards

Make your own cards by cutting and folding cover-weight paper, such as Canson Mi-Tientes, or buy quantities of boxed, blank cards. You can simply cut out and tip-mount beautiful squares of marbled paper, or you can create small collages out of woven fabric and pieces of scrap. (Which is why you should never throw away those scraps!)

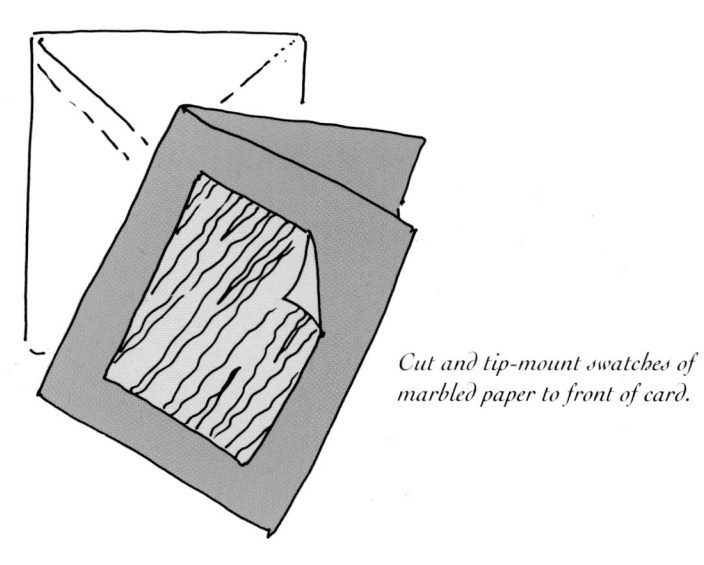

Cut and tip-mount swatches of marbled paper to front of card.

Marbling is a clever way to make personalized cards.

Accordion-fold cards are very simple to make. The cardboard pages are bound together with paper strips marbled to match the covers.

APPENDIX

Marbling as
a Business

◆

Sources

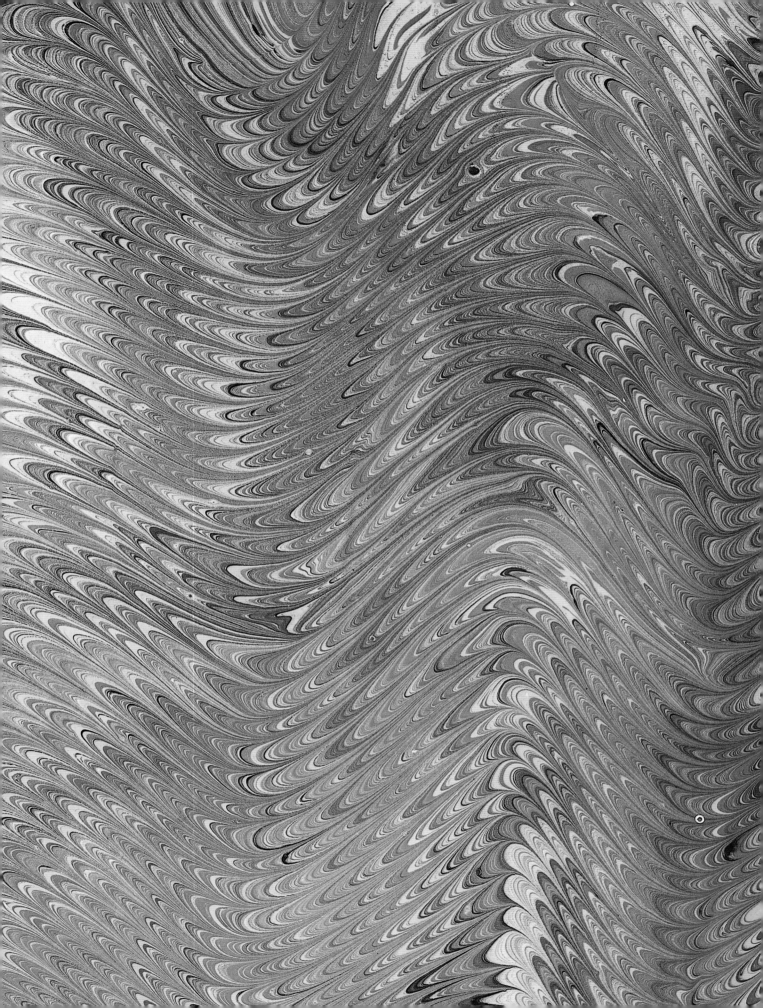

MARBLING AS A BUSINESS

There are very few marblers in this country who can truly claim that they support themselves solely through the sale of their marbled works. However, there are dozens, perhaps hundreds, who make a very good second income through the sale of their products. These artisans sell not only sheet papers, but an entire range of wonderful marbled fabric pieces and gift items. Included are greeting cards, covered boxes, lampshades, marbled pencils, T-shirts and shoes, ribbons, jewelry, silk ties, scarves, picture frames and mats, and hand-bound journals and portfolios. These objects sell very well in the gift market.

∧ *Put as much information on your papers as possible. If you use a rubber stamp, make sure your ink won't bleed through the paper into the design.*

< *A Nonpariel pattern.*

If you are interested in selling your own line of marbled goods, take them around first to gift stores and stationery stores near your home. Have an easy-to-read price list with wholesale and suggested retail prices, along with quantity discounts. Include information on shipping, delivery, and payment terms. Keep your prices as reasonable as possible to get in the door; as your business takes off, you should be able to raise them. If you want to expand out of your area, send photographs or samples of your work to selected outlets.

If you feel that you are ready and would like to reach a much larger market, buy a booth space at one of the large trade shows held yearly throughout the country. A few good ones to think about would be the American Craft Council shows, the Stationery shows in New York, and the Gift shows in New York and San Francisco. You should only do a show, however, if you are prepared to fill quantity orders and have a studio which is able to handle production work.

There is an entirely different market for the sale of sheet papers and marbled designs. The way to sell papers is primarily through art-supply stores. There is usually at least one large art-supply store in every city in this country, and it should have a comprehensive paper department. Most of these supply stores will be happy to consider selling your original marbled papers at a 100-percent markup.

Many of the customers who buy papers in art-supply stores are doing so for the purpose of using the designs in commercial art projects of one kind or another—in advertising, photography (for a backdrop), package design, and book and brochure design. I'm sure that all the readers of this book have seen the many uses of marbled papers in graphic design. They are currently being used everywhere from the Kleenex box to perfume bottles and wine labels.

When a graphic designer buys a sheet of marbled paper for $10, one of the first things that he or she will do is turn the marbled paper over to see if it has been stamped with a copyright notice. If there is no notice anywhere on that marbled paper, he or she will have no way of knowing how to reach the artist and may end up using that paper without paying any fee or giving any acknowledgement to the artist. However, most marbling artists in this country have now begun to stamp every sheet that leaves their studio with a copyright notice. The copyright stamp by itself offers no solid protection—one must follow up by registering the design with the copyright office within five years. This will legally protect you and should prevent anyone from ever using your marbled paper in any printed or reproduced way without your permission. The copyright stamp should be worded in the following manner: Copyright © 1994, Jane Smith, Larktown, Missouri. That is, you should have the word "copyright," the year, your name, and the location. An added protection would be also to stamp your papers "All Rights Reserved." Another wise move is to include your area code and phone number so that the user can call you and find out what fee you charge for the use of your paper.

Fees for usage should start at a reasonable amount, especially if you

LICENSE FOR PUBLICATION RIGHTS

Jane Smith
Fine Marbled Papers
1234 Vista Drive
Larktown, MO 94673
(314) 223-4660

This is to certify that _____ has permission to use my marbled paper for publication in the form of _____

for client_____

address and phone _____

_____

It is understood that this agreement gives permission to reproduce this paper for the above stated purpose only and in no way gives permission to reproduce in sheet form. The fee for this usage is _____. This fee applies to one marbled design only and is for a one-time publication, unless otherwise noted. A copy of the published work must also be sent to the above address for my files.

Please sign and return one copy to me, and keep the other copy for your records.

SIGNED: Marbler: _____

                 Client: _____

are a beginner. A $50 to $100 fee is a good starting point. You must find out from exact information about the project that the person contacting you is working on, before you quote a price. Get the client's name, and determine how many copies will be produced and whether a second printing or set of copies will be produced at a later date. Once you have some pertinent information about the project you will be able to set a reasonable fee. Your fee schedule should run anywhere from $50 to $1000, depending on the project and the clients. Try to keep in mind that the percentage of their budget that they are paying to you should be roughly commensurate to the percentage of artistic contribution that you are making to their project. In other words, if this is going to be a magazine ad sized about 8 x 10", and their total budget is going to be $1,000, and if you are going to supply a one square inch piece of marbled paper, then you should probably be asking for only a small amount of money. On the other hand, if the entire advertisement is covered with your marbled pattern, and it constitutes the main design element, then you should get a much greater percentage of that $1,000.

At left is a sample copyright license form which you may use in your business endeavors. For complete copyright information, consult the Office of Copyrights (Government Printing Office, Washington, D.C.), or a lawyer. Should you discover an unauthorized use of your marbled design, first send a letter and a bill to the designer (or to the printer, if you must). If you get no response you must then decide whether to call a lawyer.

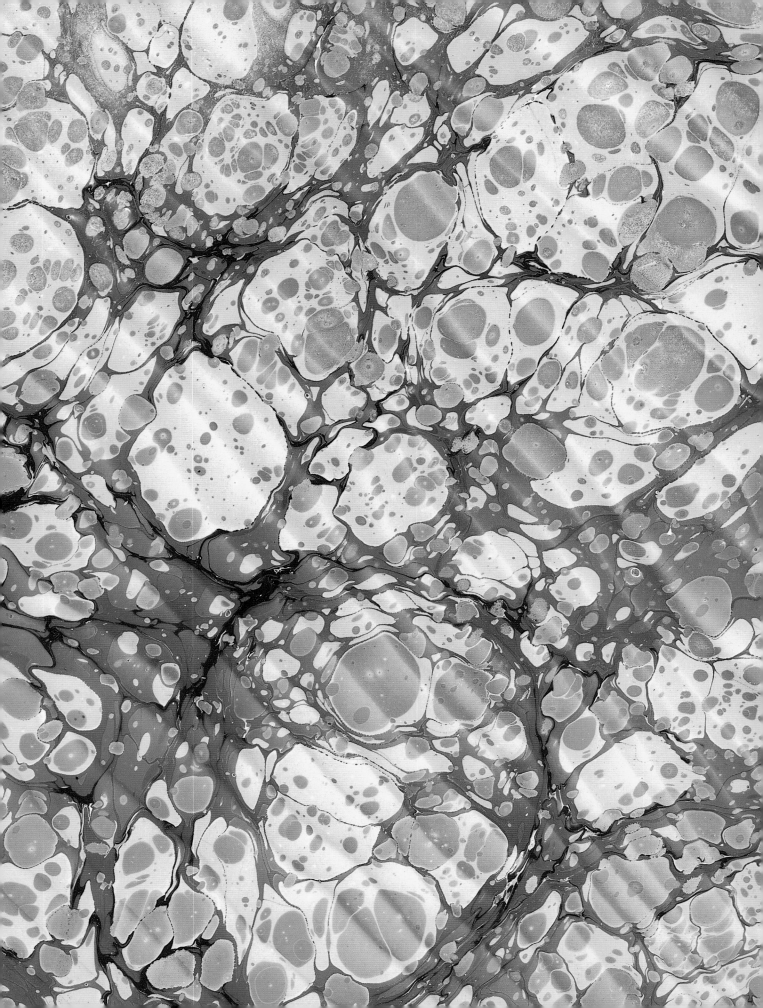

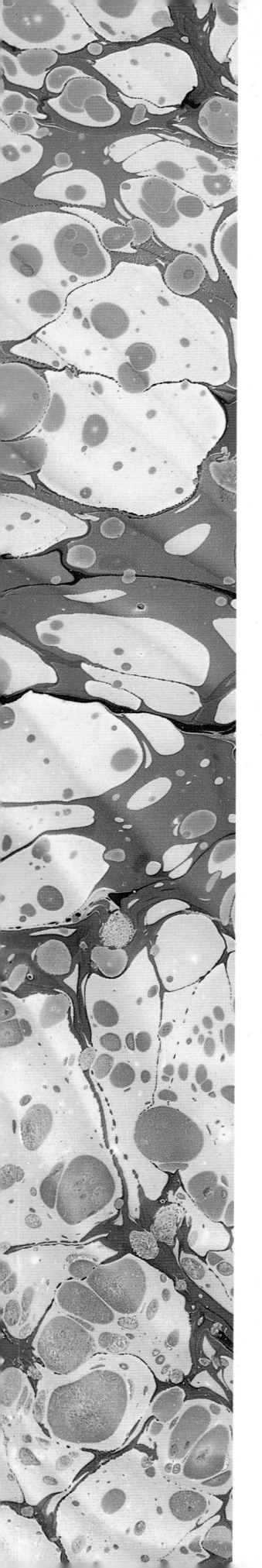

SOURCES

Amsterdam Art
1013 University Avenue
Berkeley, CA 94710
(510) 649-4800
Purveyors of the widest range of fine papers for marbling on the West Coast. Also carry marbling paints, "Instant Thickener" (methocel), Winsor & Newton Acrylic Flow Improver, bronzing powders, and related supplies for marbling.

Bryant Labs
1101 5th Street
Berkeley, CA 94710
Alum and other chemicals for artists and crafts people are available through this small but interesting outlet.

Colophon Book Arts
3046 Hogun Bay Road NE
Olympia, WA 98506
(206) 459-2940
One of the oldest businesses to serve the needs of the marbler. Carries a full line of marbling goods, including many specialized trays and tools. Catalog available.

Guild of Bookworkers
521 Fifth Avenue, 17th Floor
New York, NY 10175
Information, newsletters, seminars.

Ink and Gall
P.O. Box 1469
Taos, NM 87571
Publishers of the only magazine devoted solely to marbling, and also a wonderful resource for any kind of information, this organization also has the most complete selection of books on marbling and related arts in the United States. Ink and Gall also sells supplies for marbling. Catalog available.

New York Central Supply
62 Third Avenue
New York, NY 10003
1 (800) 950-6111
Suppliers of a wide range of paints and papers of interest to marblers. Also carry a comprehensive selection of hand-marbled papers from around the world. Catalog available.
Store #212 - 473-7705

Qualin Silks
P.O. Box 31145
San Francisco, CA 94131
Fine silks of every weave, texture, and weight. Also sell pre-hemmed silk scarves and will sew your marbled fabric into neckties. Reasonable price list.

Savoir-Faire
P.O. Box 2021
Sausalito, CA 94966
(415) 332-4660 884 - 8090
Distributors of Portfolio marbling paints, broom corn, "Instant Thickeners" (methocel), alum, marbling kits, Sennelier oil paints, Texticolor Opaque and Texticolor Iridescent paints for marblers, and hundreds of imported French mold-made and handmade papers for marbling, including Lanaquarelle Ingres and Laid Finish papers.

Daniel Smith
4128 1st Street
Seattle, WA 98134
1 (800) 426-6740
Great selection of artist papers and general art supplies, specializes in mail order.

Talas
213 West 35th Street
New York, NY 10001
(212) 736-7744
Extensive selections of traditional marbling tools and materials, along with a world-class selection of marbled papers for sale.

INDEX

NOTE: Numbers in *italics* signify illustrations.

Acrylic flow medium, 51, 60, *72*, 118
Acrylics, 51, 58-61
Addison, Julie, *26, 27*
Air bubbles, 100, 120
Alum, 48-50, 118-119
American Craft Council shows, 138
Amsterdam Art, 141
Antique Dutch (French Snail) pattern, *94*, 94-95
Antique Spot (Zebra) pattern, 40, *88*, 88
Art-supply stores, as sales outlet, 138

Back and Forth (Get-gel) pattern, *86*, 86-87, *121*
Bookbinding, marbled, 130-131
Borders, marbled, 110
Bouquet (Peacock) pattern, *92*, 92-93, *96*, 97
Boxes, marbled, 126-127
Bronzing powders, 55, 69
Broom corn whisks, 40-42, 83, 99
Brushes
    broom corn, 40
    drop, 68
    paint, 42
Bryant Labs, 141

Carragheen size, 46, 55, 61, 65
Children, marbling with, *72*, 124-125
Colophon Book Arts, 141
Colored paper, 55, 111
Color mixing, 52-55
Color wheel, 53
Combs, 42, 82, 90
Copyright, 138, 139
Cornstarch size, 46, 72-73, 124
Cove, *29*
Curlicue (French Snail) pattern, *94*, 94-95
Curtain pattern, 12, *13*, *89*, 89

Daniel Smith, 141
Drying racks, 50, *77*

Ebru (cloud art), 9
Eyedropper, 43
Eyes of color, 103

Fabric marbling, 38, 82, 116-120
Faded patches, 102
Fade-outs, 114
Fee for usage, 138-139
Filmy surface, 98
Flammable materials, 69

Florentine marbling, 10
Flower marbling, 105, 108-109
French Shell pattern, *11*
French Snail pattern, *81*, *94*, 94-95

Gesso, 50, 115
Get-gel (Back and Forth) pattern, *86*, 86-87, *121*
Gift shows, 138
Gouache, 51, 62-65
Graphic design, marbled papers in, 128
Greeting cards, marbled, 132-133
Guild of Bookworkers, 141

Iceberg shapes, 99, 102
Ink and Gall, 141
Inks, 69
Iridescent paints, 55
Irish moss. *See* Carragheen
Ironing wrinkled paper, 50

Lanaquarelle paper, 48, 64

Machado, Fernando, 17, *18-19*, *36*, 37
Manila paper, 72, 124
Marbling
    acrylics, 59-61
    antique, 11-15
    as business, 137-139
    history of, 9, 10
    materials, 45-57
    oils, 66-69
    suppliers, 141
    tempera, 70-73
    tools, 37-43
    watercolor/gouache, 62-65
Marbling process, 11, 79-133
    borders, 110
    on colored paper, 111
    fabric marbling, 38, 82, 116-120
    fade-outs/vignettes, 114
    flower marbling, 105, 108-109
    on objects, 115
    stencil marbling, 10, 26, 112-113
    technical problems in, 97-103
    See also Pattern making
Marbling projects, 122-133
    bookbinding, 130-131
    boxes, 126-127
    with children, 72, 124-125
    greeting cards, 132-133
    picture mats, 128-129

Materials, 45-57, 141
Metallic paints, 55, 69
Methocel size, 46, 61
Mineral spirits, 67, 68
Mordant, 48, 48-50, 49-50, 60, 64, 102, 118
Muddled design, 100

New York Central Supply, 141
Nonpareil pattern, *90*, 90-91, *91, 136*

Objects, marbled, 115
Oil paints, 51, 66-69
Olaf, *28*, 29, *30-33, 104*, 105
Ox gall, 51, 64

Paints, 51-55
    acrylic, 60
    applying, 98, 99
    clumps of, 103
    color mixing, 52-55
    containers for, 43
    on fabrics, 118
    faded patches, 102
    gouache, 64
    iridescent, 55
    metallic, 55, 69
    oils, 68
    sinkage, 98-99
    spreading agents, 51-52, 64, 72
    storing, 43, 55
    tempera, 71
    temperature of, 94, 99
Paper
    colored, 55, 111
    for greeting cards, 132
    ironing wrinkled sheets of, 50
    laying down, 100, 101
    manila, 72, 124
    mordant treated, 48-50, 64, 102
    selecting, 48-49, 64, 68-69
Paper, marbled
    copyrighting, 138, 139
    fees for usage, 138-139
    sales market for, 138
Pastel colors, 52, 55, *57*
Pattern making, 81-95
    Antique Spot (Zebra), 40, *88*, 88
    Back and Forth (Get-gel), *86*, 86-87, *121*
    Curtain, *89*
    French Shell, *11*
    French Snail, *81, 94*, 94-95
    Nonpareil, *90*, 90-91, *91, 136*
    Peacock (Bouquet), *92*, 92-93, *97*
    Spanish Wave, 12, *13, 14*, 15, 105, *106-107*, 106
    Turkish Stone, 40, *80*, 81, *82*, 82-85
    Peacock (Bouquet) pattern, *92*, 92-93, *97*
Picture mats, marbled, 128-129
Portfolio, marbled, 123
Portfolio paint, 51, 60, 120
Poster paint, 71

Qualin Silks, 141

Rakes, 42, 90
Rinsing station, 76-77

Safety precautions, 69
Savoir-Faire, 141
Sennelier paint, 68
Silk, marbled, 118-120
Sink, *76*
Sinking paint, 98-99
Size base
    for acrylic, 61
    bubbles on surface of, 101
    dirty, 98-99, 100
    removing, 85
    skimming off, 98
    for tempera, 72-73
    temperature of, 94, 99, 102
    tips for using, 46-47, 99
    for watercolor/gouache, 65
Soap, as spreading agent, 72
Spanish Wave pattern, 12, *13, 14*, 15, 105, *106-107*, 106
Spoons, slotted, 42
Spray nozzle, 76
Spreading agents, 51-52, 64, 72
Star shapes, 99, 102
Stationery shows, 138
Stencil marbling, 10, 26, 112-113
Stylus, *43*, 82, 105
Suppliers, 141

Talas, 141
Talens paint, 64
Tempera, 70-73
Temperature, of size and paints, 94, 99, 102
Texticolor Iridescent paint, 55
Texticolor Opaque paint, 60, 118, 120
Tools, 37-43, 141
Trade shows, 138
Trays, 38-39, 119, 124
Turkish Stone pattern, 40, *80*, 81, *82*, 82-85
Turpentine, 51, 67, 68

Vano Blue starch, 72, 124
Venetian marbling, 10
Ventilation system, 69
Victorian marbling, *8, 9*, 15
Vignettes, 114

Watercolor, 63-65
Weimann, Christopher, *16, 17*
Whisks, broom corn, 40-42, 83, 99
White areas, 100
White spots, 101
White streaks, 101
Winsor & Newton paints, 64, 68
Workspace
    drying racks, *77*
    floor covering, 75
    layout, 76
    rinsing station, *76-77*
    ventilation system in, 69

Zebra (Antique Spot) pattern, 40, *88*, 88